# SEXUAL INTEGRITY

# 101

an 8-week study for men, women, & churches

**Sexual Integrity 101 Workbook**

Copyright © 2020 by Pure Desire Ministries International

Published by
Pure Desire Ministries International
886 NW Corporate Drive, Troutdale, OR 97060
www.puredesire.org | 503.489.0230
ISBN 978-1-943291-79-3

1st Edition, August 2020

Content editing by Heather Kolb

Cover design, interior design, and typesetting by Elisabeth Windsor

# CONTENTS

# SPEAKERS

**Ashley Jameson** shines as a mentor and teacher. Since age sixteen, she has polished her leadership skills in ministry with people of all ages. Ashley and her husband have experienced, firsthand, the restoration that Pure Desire offers. In 2013, she introduced and began facilitating PD groups in her church. As the International Groups Coordinator for Pure Desire, Ashley trains new group leaders around the world. She is a contributing author to *Unraveled: Managing Love, Sex, and Relationships.*

**Heather Kolb** spent several years as a college professor before joining the Pure Desire team as a speaker, author, and editor. She holds a Bachelor of Science in psychology and Master of Science in criminal behavior. Heather is passionate about educating people on the brain and how it contributes to behavior. She co-authored *Digital Natives: Raising an Online Generation* and *Unraveled: Managing Love, Sex, and Relationships.*

**Nick Stumbo** is the Executive Director of Pure Desire and former Lead Pastor at East Hills Alliance Church. Nick earned a bachelor in Pastoral Ministry from Crown College and a Master of Divinity from Bethel University. Nick and his wife, Michelle, have helped many men and women in the church find restoration from brokenness. Nick wrote the books, *Setting Us Free* and *Safe,* to help others find help, hope, and healing.

**Robert Vander Meer** is the Associate Pastor at The Oregon Community and is a Pastoral Sex Addiction Professional (PSAP) at Pure Desire Ministries. He also is one of the founders of the Oregon Public House, a not-for-profit restaurant. Robert and his wife, Rebecca, are the owners of Woodlawn Swap 'n Play, a community-focused play space. They live in community and care deeply about being vulnerable and visible to others.

# EXPERTS

**Ben Bennett** currently serves with Josh McDowell Ministry as an author, speaker, and the Director of The Resolution Movement—a new national initiative helping youth overcome hurts, unwanted behaviors, and live a thriving life. Ben co-authored *Living Free*, a resource to help young men find freedom from unwanted sexual behavior. He holds a bachelor's degree in art and visual technology from George Mason University. He resides in Dallas, Texas, and enjoys traveling, music, and investing in his relationships.

**Jay Stringer** is a licensed mental health counselor, ordained minister, and author of the award-winning book *Unwanted: How Sexual Brokenness Reveals Our Way to Healing*. He holds an MDiv and master in counseling psychology from the Seattle School of Theology and Psychology. He received post-graduate training under Dr. Dan Allender as a Senior Fellow at the Allender Center. His passion is to equip the church with resources to change the conversation on sexual brokenness. Jay and his wife have two children and live in New York, New York.

**Dr. Juli Slattery** is a clinical psychologist, author, speaker, and the president/co-founder of Authentic Intimacy—a ministry devoted to reclaiming God's design for sexuality. Juli earned her college degree at Wheaton College, an MA in psychology from Biola University, and an MS and a Doctorate degree in Clinical Psychology from Florida Institute of Technology. Juli is the author of ten books, including *Rethinking Sexuality*. She is also the host of the weekly podcast "Java with Juli." Juli and her husband Mike have three sons and they live in Akron, Ohio.

**Mo Isom** is a New York Times Best-Selling author and speaker who is a part of BOLDLIFE INITIATIVE, a ministry that exists to challenge, encourage, and equip Christ followers to relentlessly pursue holy and BOLD lives. She is the author of *Sex, Jesus, And The Conversations The Church Forgot* and the New York Times Best-Seller *Wreck My Life*. She uses her degree in Mass Communication from LSU to support her passion in courageously communicating the full Gospel with raw authenticity, compassion, and fresh revelation. Mo and her husband live in Atlanta, Georgia with their three children.

# INTRODUCTION

For men and women who struggle with unwanted sexual behaviors, the weight of their shame and guilt is relentless. They feel isolated and alone, certain no one else struggles like they do.

For the spouse who has experienced betrayal, the devastation of being promised again and again that things would be different—and they're not—is overwhelming. They are trapped by the trauma they are living every day.

And for those who struggle with unhealthy relationship patterns, they genuinely want to develop healthy relationships, but don't know where to start.

*Sexual Integrity 101* is an 8-week training course intended to raise awareness of sexual brokenness. It's for men, women, students, pastors, lay leaders, parents, and more—anyone who wants to find freedom from the effects of unwanted sexual behaviors and betrayal.

## THROUGHOUT THIS COURSE, WE WILL LEARN ABOUT:

- ➔ the role shame plays in unwanted sexual behavior and how grace influences the healing process.
- ➔ how pain and trauma affect our brain and how we can create new, healthy neural pathways.
- ➔ the resources, tools, and daily practices needed to start a personal healing journey or start a healing ministry in your church.
- ➔ how sexual brokenness affects relationships and how, when we get healthy, relationships can be transformed
- ➔ how to heal the wounds of our past in a safe, grace-filled community.

We believe that through the Holy Spirit and the training in this course, we can not only start the conversation, but equip men, women, and churches in developing sexual integrity.

Together, we can change the tide of sexual brokenness in our world.

# HOW TO LEAD A 101 GROUP

## 01. PURCHASE SEXUAL INTEGRITY 101:

either in a digital or physical (DVD) copy.

## 02. SET UP A MEETING TIME.

You will need approximately 1.5-2 hours of time for each session.

## 03. ALL GROUP MEMBERS WILL NEED A WORKBOOK.

Look for bulk discounts when purchasing for a group.

## 04. MEET ONCE PER WEEK OVER AN 8-WEEK PERIOD.

If meeting in a small group, in person or online, there should be no more than 10 group members. This allows the group to get through the session content in a timely manner.

If meeting in a large group, in person or online, the number of attendees/viewers is unlimited. However, when going through the reflection questions, the attendees/viewers should be split into smaller groups of no more than 10 members.

**During each weekly meeting, use this proposed time outline:**

- Watch session content: 35-50 minutes
- Individually, fill out the Reflection Questions: 10-15 minutes
- As a group, talk through the Reflection Questions: 30-45 minutes

## 05. EACH GROUP MEMBER SHOULD COMPLETE THE WEEKLY WORK BETWEEN EACH MEETING.

This is where the group members will put into practice what they are learning throughout the video course. This will also prepare them for the following week's discussion.

**We recommend all groups follow the PD Group Guidelines and members sign the Memo of Understanding found on pages 142-143 in the Appendix.**

# Session 01.

# DIFFERENT THAN EXPECTED

When it comes to understanding unwanted sexual behavior, many people would naturally think the primary issue is about sex. But more often than not, sexual brokenness is a symptom of something much deeper.

As we will learn in this session, there are many factors that contribute to sexual brokenness. We will also see why it's such a challenging topic to discuss and why so many men and women struggle in silence.

When it comes to the sexual landscape of our world, many of us have found ourselves in a place very different than we expected.

_____

_____

_____

_____

_____

_____

_____

_____

# THE REALITY

We are being inundated by sexual content! It's estimated that:

**68%** of Christian men struggle with unwanted sexual behavior.[1]

**25-30%** Christian women struggle with sexual dependency issues.[2]

**57%** of pastors have a current or past struggle with pornography.[3]

**91%** of men and **60%** of women had accessed pornography in the last 30 days.[4]

**56%**

of divorces involve the internet use of a partner as a driving factor.[5]

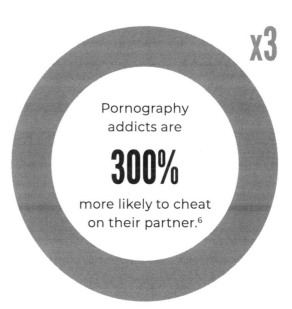

x3

Pornography addicts are

**300%**

more likely to cheat on their partner.[6]

## "IT SEEMS SO OBVIOUS: IF WE INVENT A MACHINE, THE FIRST THING WE ARE GOING TO DO AFTER MAKING A PROFIT IS USE IT TO WATCH PORN.

#### DAMON BROWN[7]

---

[1] Ongoing data collected by Pure Desire Ministries International, 2009-present. Participants of study completing SAST-R, V2.0 © 2008, P.J. Carnes, Sexual Addiction Screening Test-Revised.

[2] Ibid.

[3] Josh McDowell Ministry (2016). *The Porn Phenomenon: The Impact of Pornography in the Digital Age*. Ventura, CA: Barna Group.

[4] Solano, I., Eaton, N. & O'Leary, K. (2018). Pornography Consumption, Modality and Function in a Large Internet Sample. *The Journal of Sex Research*, 57:1, 92-103, DOI: 10.1080/00224499.2018.1532488

[5] Covenant Eyes (2018). *Porn Stats: 250+ facts, quotes, and statistics about pornography use*. Owosso, MI: Covenant Eyes, Inc. 13.

[6] Fagan, P. (2009). The Effects of Pornography on Individuals, Marriage, Family, and Community. *Marriage & Religion Research Institute*. December. 8.

[7] Ibid. 5.

# THE FOUR "A"S OF PORNOGRAPHY

- ➡ **Affordable:** the majority of pornography is free online.
- ➡ **Available:** pornography is easily accessible—anything, anytime, anywhere.
- ➡ **Anonymous:** we don't have to be known or leave the privacy of our home to use pornography.
- ➡ **Aggressive:** pornography is more violent than ever.

> THE PORN PARADOX: NEVER BEFORE HAS PORNOGRAPHY BEEN MORE POPULAR, BUT AT THE SAME TIME, NEVER BEFORE HAS IT BEEN MORE VIOLENT.

> "ANY PORN USE IS ASSOCIATED WITH DECLINES IN RELIGIOUS COMMITMENT AND BEHAVIOR AND AN INCREASE IN RELIGIOUS DOUBTS."
>
> DR. SAMUEL PERRY[8]

How did we get here? The truth is that we are all being exposed and impacted by pornography and sexual brokenness around us. Even if we have never personally struggled, we are impacted through relationships—we have friends, family members, and spouses who struggle. We all know people who have been victims of abuse, hurt by someone else's unprocessed sexual issues.

We simply can't ignore this problem and hope it gets better. We must be equipped to be part of the solution, whether for our own story or to play a role in someone else's story.

---

[8] Perry, S.L. (2017). Does Viewing Pornography Diminish Religiosity Over Time? Evidence From Two-Wave Panel Data. The Journal of Sex Research, 54:2, 214-226. DOI: 10.1080/00224499.2016.1146203.

# EVERYONE IS SEXUALLY BROKEN.
### JULI SLATTERY

# PUSH-PULL

There is a unique push-pull of unwanted sexual behavior that so many of us feel. We feel the pull of desire and pleasure and the push of hating the behaviors we continue doing.

This push-pull is what creates a very unique place of shame in our souls. This can create a framework in our thinking that sex is very shameful and secret.

# THE POWER OF PAIN

Pain can be a powerful motivator when changing behavior.

_____
_____
_____
_____
_____
_____
_____
_____
_____

## MARRIAGE DOESN'T CHANGE YOU, IT JUST REVEALS MORE OF WHAT IT FINDS.
### RODNEY WRIGHT

# FIVE STAGES OF SEXUALLY COMPULSIVE BEHAVIOR

**01.** Early Exposure

**02.** Escalating Struggle

**03.** Detesting and Desiring

**04.** Failed Attempts to Stop

**05.** Relationship Issues

# DEFINING ADDICTION

When it comes to the challenge of defining "addiction," we too often focus on the degree of behavior. For example, if someone is just using fantasy or online pornography, it's not an addiction, it's a struggle. But, someone who is paying for sex or visiting strip clubs, which is extreme behavior, has an addiction. The degree of behavior really doesn't tell the whole story.

Addiction is much more about "**dependence**" and "**disturbance**."

_____

_____

_____

_____

_____

# DETERMINING AN ADDICTION

> **?**
>
> 01. How long has this been a problem?
> 02. How many times have you tried to stop?
> 03. Is it causing you or people you love significant amounts of pain?

_____

_____

_____

_____

_____

_____

> ## WE (THE CHURCH) ARE SIMPLY SPEAKING TO THE SYMPTOMS RATHER THAN PULLING BACK AND ADDRESSING THE HEART ISSUE AT THE ROOT OF SEXUAL BROKENNESS.
>
> MO ISOM

# GOING BELOW THE SURFACE

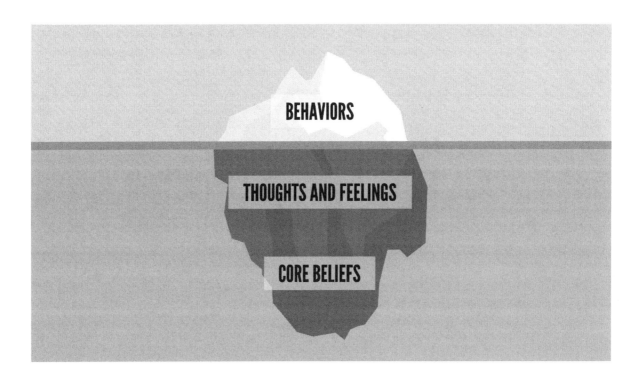

We behave in accordance with how we think and feel. What we think about often enough and long enough is what we tend to do and become.

Changing our behaviors is not enough. We need to recognize how our core beliefs lead to our thoughts and feelings which lead to our actions. This is why simply trying harder doesn't work.

# THE CYCLONE OF ADDICTION

We might refer to our struggle with unwanted sexual behaviors like a cyclone: a damaging storm that can cause serious issues in our world. For a cyclone to form, there must be several factors in the environment: air temperature; a hot and a cold front meeting; wind speed; and more. All of these factors must be present or a cyclone will not form.

This is also true in The Cyclone of Addiction. A number of factors must be present that contribute to our addictive behaviors. As we work through these factors, one by one, we will begin to see The Cyclone of Addiction dissipating and losing its power.

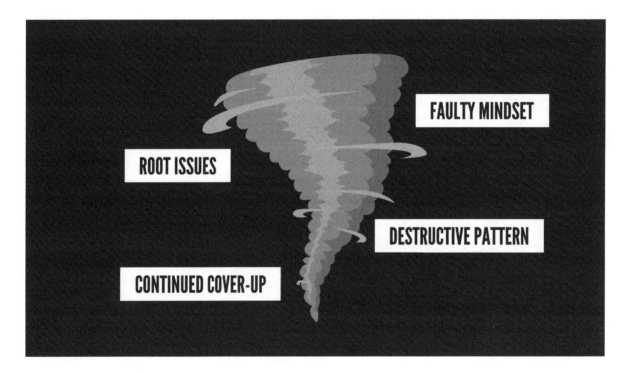

## ROOT ISSUES

- Family of origin dysfunction
- Early abuse and personal trauma
- Growing up in an addictive society

# FAULTY MINDSET

➲ Core beliefs of unworthiness or shame

➲ Discomfort with feeling alone

➲ False concept of need for sex

# DESTRUCTIVE PATTERN[9]

➲ Preoccupation

➲ Ritualization

➲ Compulsion

➲ Despair

# CONTINUED COVER-UP

➲ Denial

➲ Rationalizing

➲ Minimizing

➲ Delusion

➲ Blaming others

No matter what your personal struggle or what brought you here, this journey will be life-changing!

We may be at a place very different than we expected, but God wants to meet us in a very real way right where we're at, regardless of our struggle. God wants to work in us so that He can work through us.

> *Then your salvation will come like the dawn, and your wounds will quickly heal. Your godliness will lead you forward, and the glory of the Lord will protect you from behind...Then you will be known as a rebuilder of walls and a restorer of homes.*
>
> **ISAIAH 58:8,12 NLT**

---

[9] Carnes, P. (2000). Sexual Addiction and Compulsion: Recognition, Treatment & Recovery. *CNS Spectrums*, 5(10), 63-72.

# Session 01.
# REFLECTION QUESTIONS

**?** | When it comes to the sexual landscape of our world, many of us have found ourselves in a place very different than we expected. In what way(s) is this statement true in your life?

_____

_____

_____

_____

_____

**?** | What do you think and/or feel when hearing the statistics provided in this session?

_____

_____

_____

_____

**?** How are The Four "A"s of Pornography and The Porn Paradox changing the way you think personally and how we think culturally?

_____
_____
_____
_____
_____
_____

**?** Whether you are the one struggling or have been impacted by someone's struggle, how has pornography affected your relationship with God and others?

_____
_____
_____
_____
_____
_____

**?** How does the clinical definition of addiction help to make sense of your behaviors or the behaviors you've observed in others?

_____
_____
_____
_____
_____
_____
_____

**?** | How do you want to become part of the solution in your own story?
In someone else's story?

_____
_____
_____
_____
_____
_____

**?** | Pain can be a powerful motivator when it comes to changing behavior.
When has God allowed pain in your life to create great change in your heart?

_____
_____
_____
_____
_____
_____

**?** | In what ways does understanding the Cyclone of Addiction give hope for
the healing process?

_____
_____
_____
_____
_____
_____

# Session 01.
# WEEKLY WORK

## REALITY CHECK

Take some time to journal about your current reality and what you hope to see God do over the course of this study.

# BELOW THE SURFACE EXERCISE

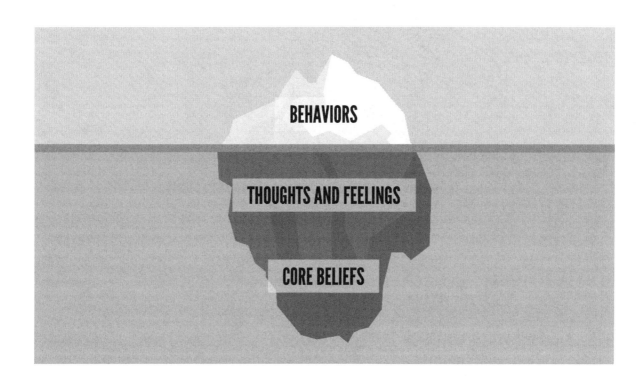

**?** What behaviors have you tried to change—those above the surface?

_____

_____

_____

_____

_____

_____

_____

_____

_____

**?** What thoughts and feelings drive your behaviors—
those just below the surface?

_____

_____

_____

_____

_____

_____

_____

_____

_____

_____

**?** What core beliefs contribute to your thoughts and feelings—
things you believe about yourself? (e.g., I'm unworthy. I'm undeserving.
I'm not good enough.)

_____

_____

_____

_____

_____

_____

_____

_____

_____

_____

_____

_____

# Session 02.

# A CULTURE OF GRACE

For the many men and women struggling with unwanted sexual behaviors, shame is a primary reason they stay stuck. Shame becomes their shackles—holding them in bondage and making it feel impossible to escape.

In this session, we will see how our healing starts with creating a culture of grace; in our home, in our church, and in our community. Grace is the key that unlocks our hearts and makes hope, healing, and transformation possible.

How did we get here? What happened *to* us and *around* us creating a pathway that brought us to a place of sexual brokenness?

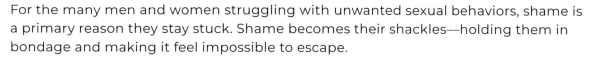

# A SECRET LIFE

For many of us who struggle with unwanted sexual behaviors, we end up living a double life. The life we allow others to see: successful at our job, happily married, great parent, strong community, and more. Then we have this other life, fueled by shame and secrecy, that slowly erodes every aspect of our world.

> ## OUR UNWANTED BEHAVIORS, EVEN THE SPECIFIC FANTASIES WE SEARCH FOR ON THE INTERNET, ARE NOT RANDOM AT ALL. THEY CAN BE SHAPED AND PREDICTED BY THE PARTS OF OUR STORY THAT REMAIN UNADDRESSED.
>
> ### JAY STRINGER

---
---
---
---
---
---
---
---
---
---

# ASKING FOR HELP

Too often, even when we ask for help, we find that many people don't have the tools or the ability to help others struggling with unwanted sexual behaviors.

# THE WORLD IS MORE THAN WILLING TO RAISE THEIR VOICE ABOUT SEX.

### MO ISOM

This is not only a problem for the Church. It's a problem in our homes, schools, and society. There are plenty of stories of sexual brokenness in the world around us.

> *Jesus was still angry as he arrived at the tomb, a cave with a stone rolled across its entrance. "Roll the stone aside," Jesus told them.*
>
> *But Martha, the dead man's sister, protested, "Lord, he has been dead for four days. The smell will be terrible."*
>
> ### JOHN 11:38-39 NLT

---
---
---
---
---
---

Jesus is saying, "Let's take a look inside this tomb of death, where there's brokenness, where there's pain, where everything that Lazarus' death represents is in there."

Jesus is saying, "Let's roll the stone away," and Lazarus' family is saying, "We don't want to see it. We can't handle it. We don't want to be exposed to what's in there."

---
---
---
---
---
---

> *Jesus responded, "Didn't I tell you that you would see God's glory if you believe?" So they rolled the stone aside. Then Jesus looked up to heaven and said, "Father, thank you for hearing me. You always hear me, but I said it out loud for the sake of all these people standing here, so that they will believe you sent me." Then Jesus shouted, "Lazarus, come out!" And the dead man came out, his hands and feet bound in graveclothes, his face wrapped in a head cloth. Jesus told them, "Unwrap him and let him go!"*

## JOHN 11:38-44 NLT

_____

_____

_____

_____

_____

_____

## " I KNEW JESUS WAS CALLING ME INTO THE LIGHT BECAUSE IT'S BETTER IN THE LIGHT, HOWEVER, I WAS AFRAID OF THE PEOPLE OUT THERE IN THE LIGHT. "

How often does our shame and fear keep us from walking into the light, even when we hear Jesus calling us?

# GRACE & COMPETENCY

If we expect people to ask for help, they need to be met with two things: grace and competency.

Grace says, "I love you for who you are, not for what you've done."

Competency is the ability to help them.

If there's not grace and competency in whatever our context is, people are more likely to stay in isolation and their tomb of death than they are to walk out into the light. This is a cultural problem, not just an individual problem.

# THE CYCLONE OF ADDICTION

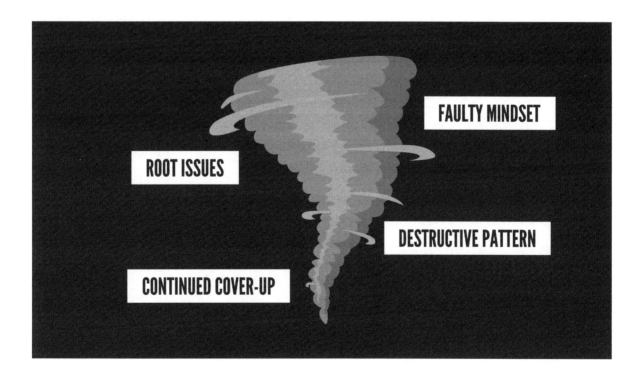

# THE POWER OF SHAME

One of the most important pieces to The Cyclone of Addiction is the toxic power of shame. If shame isn't present, the cyclone dies.

Grace is the antidote for shame.

When creating a Culture of Grace, we need to minimize the level of shame. Without shame, the storm's driving force is gone.

It's important to identify the difference between guilt and shame.

## GUILT SAYS, "I DID BAD." SHAME SAYS, "I AM BAD."

_____

_____

_____

_____

_____

_____

_____

_____

Unwanted sexual behavior has more to do with pain and fear than it has to do with sex itself. We all experience pain in our lives, but what we do with this pain is key.

# WE HAVE TWO OPTIONS:

**01.** Process our pain with others;

OR

**02.** Numb the pain.

If we try to numb the pain, what we're really doing is adding pleasure to it, which creates brokenness. Brokenness creates guilt and shame.

## THE SHAME CYCLE

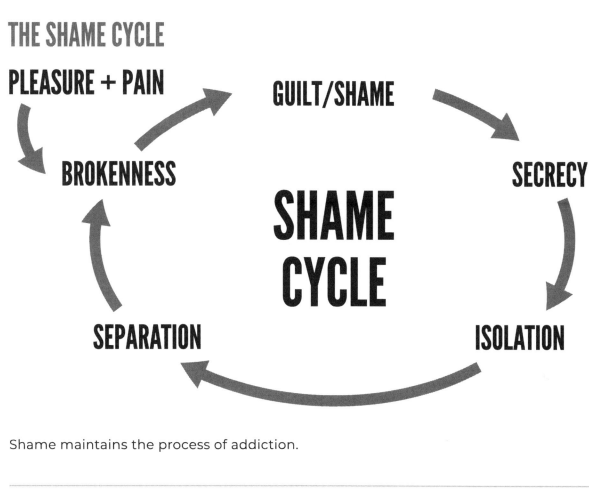

**PLEASURE + PAIN**

**GUILT/SHAME**

**SECRECY**

**SHAME CYCLE**

**BROKENNESS**

**ISOLATION**

**SEPARATION**

Shame maintains the process of addiction.

**"MANY OF US LIVE LIVES RUNNING FROM OUR SHAME. WE DON'T TURN AND FACE THOSE THINGS, THEREFORE THEY HAVE RULE AND DOMINION OVER OUR LIVES."**

JAY STRINGER

# TWO PATHWAYS OF SHAME

**01.** Unconfessed sin in our lives

**02.** Satan's lies that fuel our negative behaviors

# FOUR DIMENSIONS OF SHAME

- Shame results from broken relationships.
- Exposure makes us feel diminished.
- Fear causes us to hide.
- Creates a belief there's something wrong with me.

As shame gains momentum in our lives, it makes us behavior-focused, creating a performance-based way of looking at life.

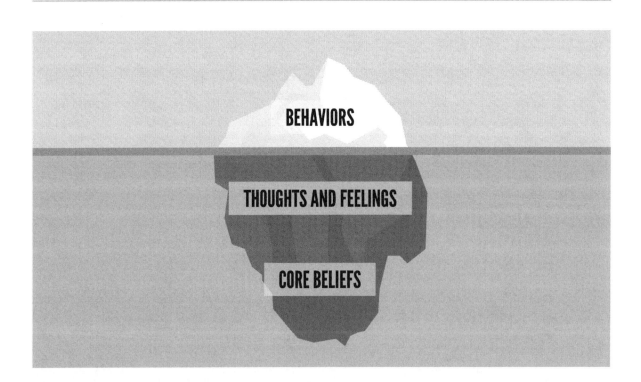

Our thoughts and feelings drive our behaviors.

> ## "THE CHURCH OFTEN EMPHASIZES THE DOING AND PERFORMING, BUT GOD IS CALLING US TO THE BEING, KNOWING, AND BECOMING."
>
> **MO ISOM**

## BEHAVING BETTER WILL NEVER LEAD TO LASTING CHANGE.

# CREATING A CULTURE OF GRACE

_____

_____

_____

_____

_____

_____

_____

Our heavenly Father offers grace apart from our performance and restores our God-given identity.

> *So now there is no condemnation for those who belong to Christ Jesus. And because you belong to him, the power of the life-giving Spirit has freed you from the power of sin that leads to death.*
>
> **ROMANS 8:1-2 NLT**

In a culture of grace, we work from a restored identity in Christ, as opposed to working for it.

_____

_____

_____

_____

_____

_____

_____

_____

# HOW TO CREATE A CULTURE OF GRACE

**01.** Cast a vision of the church as a safe place.

**02.** Give the gift of going first.

**03.** Use the power of story.

**04.** Reward honesty.

**05.** Cultivate environments for true intimacy.

**06.** Release the power of shared experience.

**07.** Stay open and honest.

If we want to change culture and create a safe place for healing, we have to change the way we do life. The change starts with us.

_____

_____

_____

_____

_____

_____

_____

_____

# Session 02.
# REFLECTION QUESTIONS

**?** | What part of Robert's story do you relate to most?

_____
_____
_____
_____
_____

**?** | How does living a double life perpetuate our sexual brokenness?

_____
_____
_____
_____
_____
_____

**?** | Why do so many people struggle with asking for help?
How does this seem to be more prevalent in the Church?

---

**?** | Like Lazarus, stepping into the light can feel scary.
How does our fear of others trump our trust in God?

---

**?** | How does shame hold us captive
and keep us stuck in unhealthy behaviors?

---

*Session 02.*

# WEEKLY WORK

# THOUGHTS/FEELINGS LOG[1]

Learning how our thoughts and feelings influence our behaviors takes time and practice. Use the following table to make connections between the thoughts and feelings that are affecting your behavior this week. Remember, there are no wrong answers.

| I FELT... | ...BECAUSE I THOUGHT... |
| --- | --- |
| *Example: disappointed* | *I was getting a promotion.* |
| *Example: excited* | *I wasn't expecting a promotion, but got one!* |
| | |
| | |
| | |
| | |
| | |

[1] Riggenbach, J. (2013). *The CBT Toolbox: A Workbook for Clients and Clinicians.*

# THE CYCLONE OF ADDICTION

**?** | What elements of The Cyclone of Addiction do you find present in your own life?

# REFLECTION QUESTION

**?** | When considering the steps to take in creating a culture of grace, what one area can you start working toward this week?

*Session 03.*

# REVISITING OUR PAST

If we want to discover what perpetuates our unwanted sexual behavior, it requires more than simply looking at the behavior. It comes from understanding the brain—how our brain develops, the environmental factors involved, and how experience shapes our brain.

In this session, we'll learn about brain structures and function and how addictive behaviors take over the reward system, reinforcing unwanted behaviors. We'll uncover why stopping the behavior is so challenging for those who struggle.

If we want to understand our behavior—why we do what we do—we have to understand what's happening in the brain.

> *Do not conform to the pattern of this world, but be transformed by the renewing of your mind. Then you will be able to test and approve what God's will is—his good, pleasing and perfect will.*
>
> **ROMANS 12:2**

_____

_____

_____

_____

_____

## NEURONS THAT FIRE TOGETHER, WIRE TOGETHER.

As we repeat behaviors over and over, this creates neural pathways in our brain that become cemented together.[1]

# THE HUMAN BRAIN[2]

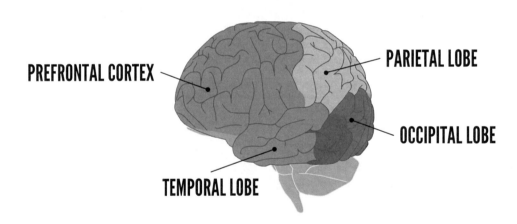

PREFRONTAL CORTEX

PARIETAL LOBE

OCCIPITAL LOBE

TEMPORAL LOBE

The **Cerebral Cortex** contains 70% of the neurons that make up our Central Nervous System and is where most of our higher mental processes take place.

The **Prefrontal Cortex** is instrumental in decision making, planning, and impulse control. This area of the brain is not fully functional until our mid-twenties.

[1] Doidge, N. (2007). *The Brain That Changes Itself: Stories of Personal Triumph from the Frontiers of Brain Science.* New York, NY: Penguin Books. 63.

[2] Ciccarelli, S. & White, J. (2012). *Psychology* (3rd ed.) Upper Saddle River, NJ: Prentice Hall. 74-76.

The **Parietal Lobe** helps us to regulate touch, temperature, pressure, and spatial awareness.

The **Occipital Lobe** helps us to interpret what our eyes are seeing.

The left side of the **Temporal Lobe** helps us process analytical thinking, speech, and reason; the right side of the Temporal Lobe helps us process emotions, dreams, and music.

The Temporal Lobe is instrumental in the development of empathy because of mirror neurons. Mirror neurons are a unique classification of neuron that allow us to learn through observation.

| **EMPATHY** | when we share the emotions of others as if we're feeling it ourselves. |
|---|---|

Many individuals who struggle with addictive behaviors lack empathy—they weren't raised in an environment where empathy was modeled for them.

_____
_____
_____
_____
_____
_____
_____
_____
_____
_____
_____
_____
_____
_____
_____

# THE LIMBIC SYSTEM[3]

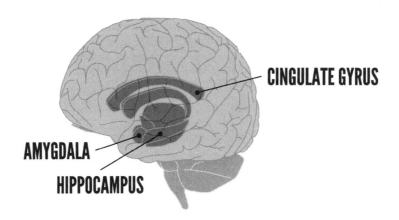

CINGULATE GYRUS

AMYGDALA

HIPPOCAMPUS

The **Limbic System** (center for emotions and memory) is in the center of our brain and is highly responsive to the neurotransmitter dopamine.

The **Hippocampus** is responsible for moving our short-term memory into long-term memory. It also helps us remember significant things that happen in our lives.

The **Amygdala** is responsible for our emotional response: anger, sadness, but especially fear. The Amygdala is activated when something happens in our environment that is out of our control.

The Hippocampus and Amygdala work together—they capture the details surrounding a specific event and how it made us feel in the moment and fuse them together in our brain.

The **Cingulate Gyrus** links our motivation and behavior. It is known as the gear-shifter of the brain, which allows us to be flexible and adaptable when we recognize that change is needed. However, when we experience trauma—something happens to us or around us that is out of our control—it makes us *not* flexible.

_____

_____

_____

_____

_____

_____

[3] Ibid. 71-72.

# EARLY CHILDHOOD DEVELOPMENT

If we want to fully understand addictive behaviors, we need to consider the role of early childhood development.

Our brain is the only organ not fully developed at birth and 90% of critical brain development happens before the age of five.[4]

Affect regulation (emotional regulation): the ability to soothe and calm ourselves when we feel stressed.

# OUR ATTACHMENT STYLE[5]

## SECURE CHILD

When the mother returned, the child went quickly to their mother, was easily comforted, and went back to playing. This child had learned that their mother was safe: they could expect their physical and emotional needs to be met in a safe environment.

## AVOIDANT CHILD

When the mother returned, the child made no attempt to go to their mother or receive any comfort. This child had learned that their mother was not safe: in order for them to survive, they needed to become independent from their mother.

## AMBIVALENT CHILD

When the mother returned, the child went to their mother and received some comfort, but then pushed their mother away. This child had learned that their mother was not safe: although she was physically present, she could not meet the child's physical and emotional needs.

---

[4] Brown, T. T., & Jernigan, T. L. (2012). Brain development during the preschool years. *Neuropsychology review*, 22(4), 313–333. https://doi.org/10.1007/s11065-012-9214-1

[5] Cozolino, L. (2014). *The Neuroscience of Human Relationships: Attachment and the Developing Social Brain* (2nd ed.). New York, NY: W. W. Norton & Company, Inc. 145-150.

## CHAOTIC/DISORGANIZED CHILD

When the mother returned, the child moved toward their mother, then stopped, and was often found on the other side of the room. This child had learned that their mother was not safe: she is the abuser.

They followed these children for the next 30 years and found that they behaved the same way in their adult relationships, especially their close intimate relationships.

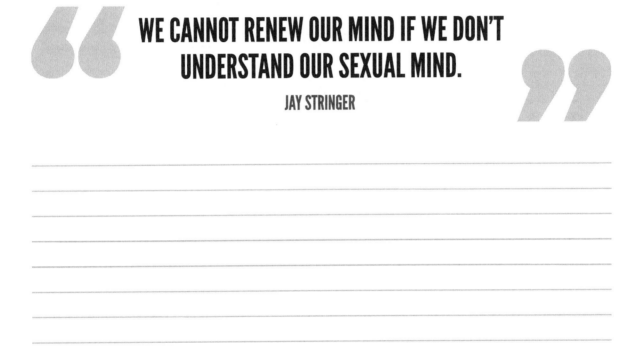

> **WE CANNOT RENEW OUR MIND IF WE DON'T UNDERSTAND OUR SEXUAL MIND.**
>
> JAY STRINGER

# THE ACEs STUDY

The ACEs Study looked at the correlation between painful and traumatic childhood experiences and adult physical and mental health issues.[6]

---

[6] Van Niel, C., Pachter, L. M., Wade, R., Jr, Felitti, V. J., & Stein, M. T. (2014). Adverse events in children: predictors of adult physical and mental conditions. *Journal of developmental and behavioral pediatrics : JDBP, 35*(8), 549–551. https://doi.org/10.1097/DBP.0000000000000102

To give you a snapshot of the data collected, compared to people with an ACEs score of zero, those with an ACEs score of four or more were:

- **2x** as likely to be smokers,
- **12x** more likely to have attempted suicide,
- **7x** more likely to be an alcoholic, and
- **10x** more likely to have injected street drugs.

Additionally, those with a higher ACEs score are more likely to experience depression, heart disease, cancer, obesity, lung disease, skeletal fractures, liver disease, and engage in promiscuous sexual behaviors.

> ## EARLY INTERPERSONAL TRAUMA IN THE FORM OF EMOTIONAL AND PHYSICAL ABUSE, SEXUAL ABUSE, AND NEGLECT SHAPE THE STRUCTURE AND FUNCTIONING OF THE BRAIN IN WAYS THAT NEGATIVELY AFFECT ALL STAGES OF SOCIAL, EMOTIONAL, AND INTELLECTUAL DEVELOPMENT.[7]

To understand our addictive patterns, we need to evaluate our family of origin and recognize how shame contributes to our addictive behaviors.

_____

_____

_____

_____

_____

_____

_____

_____

_____

[7] Cozolino, L. (2014). *The Neuroscience of Human Relationships: Attachment and the Developing Social Brain* (2nd ed.). New York, NY: W.W. Norton & Company.

# THE ADDICTIVE CYCLE[8]

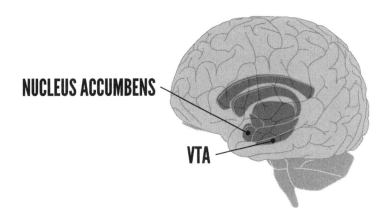

**NUCLEUS ACCUMBENS**

**VTA**

The **VTA (Ventral Tegmental Area)** is the origin of the dopamine cycle: the natural reward system in our brain. It looks for novelty and excitement in our environment, and when it finds something, it releases dopamine (a pleasure chemical in our brain).

Dopamine is sent to the **Nucleus Accumbens**, which produces intense feelings of euphoria and pleasure. Dopamine is a powerful motivator, but it can decrease brain function when our dopamine system is out of balance.

## IN A HEALTHY BRAIN

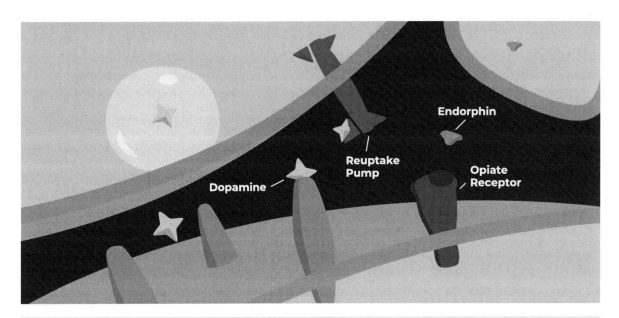

Endorphin

Reuptake
Pump

Opiate
Receptor

Dopamine

[8] Ibid. 128-129.

- The sending neuron releases dopamine into the synapse.
- The receiving neuron takes in the amount of dopamine needed to send the signal.
- The sending neuron recycles the excess dopamine through the reuptake pump.

# IN A BRAIN ON COCAINE

- The cocaine molecule enters the synapse and blocks the reuptake pump.
- The dopamine cannot be recycled and over stimulates the brain.
- The system is flooded with dopamine, which produces feelings of euphoria.

# TOLERANCE

## PROGRESSIVE DRUG TOLERANCE

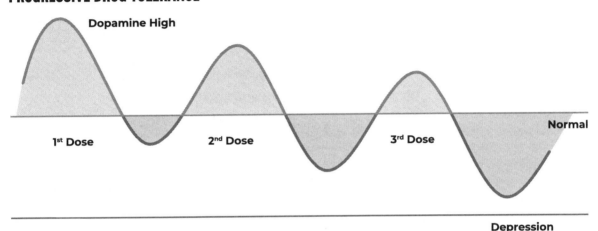

When a person starts using a substance or a behavior to stimulate the production of dopamine, the first time, they will feel a high unlike anything they've ever felt before. As their dopamine levels return to normal, they may drop below baseline and experience a bit of a depressive state. This will feel uncomfortable, so they will want to use the same substance or behavior again—trying to stimulate the production of dopamine—to feel the same high.

Unfortunately, because our brain is all about balance, our brain is already adapting to having too much dopamine. Over time, as a person uses the same behavior (or substance), they will not feel the same high. An escalation in behavior (or more of a substance) is required to get the same dopamine response.

This is tolerance.[9] When we no longer respond to a stimulus the same way and need something more risky and more taboo to produce dopamine.

Our brain responds the same way to all forms of pleasure regardless of its source.

[9] Rosenberg, K. & Feder, L. (2014). *Behavioral Addictions: Criteria, Evidence, and Treatment.* London, UK: Elsevier, Inc. 3.

> ## "I DIDN'T JUST HAVE THIS MORAL PROBLEM WITH PORNOGRAPHY AND SEXUAL SIN, BUT I HAD A DEEPLY HARD-WIRED BRAIN PROBLEM."
> BEN BENNETT

> ## "PORNOGRAPHY WASN'T ULTIMATELY MY PROBLEM, IT WAS MY PSUEDO SOLUTION."
> BEN BENNETT

_____

_____

_____

_____

_____

_____

_____

_____

_____

_____

_____

_____

> ## "UNWANTED SEXUAL BEHAVIOR IS ABOUT PURSUING BEHAVIORS THAT PROVIDE US WITH IRREFUTABLE EVIDENCE THAT WE ARE BROKEN BEYOND REPAIR."
> JAY STRINGER

# RAISING SECURE CHILDREN

Studies have shown that a parent who has processed their trauma—who can tell a coherent narrative of their history—can raise a secure child.[10]

 

[10] Iyengar, U., Kim, S., Martinez, S., Fonagy, P., and Strathearn, L. (2014). Unresolved trauma in mothers: intergenerational effects and the role of reorganization. Frontiers in Psychology, 5:966. doi: 10.3389/fpsyg.2014.00966.

# Session 03.

# REFLECTION QUESTIONS

**?** | What did you learn about the brain that provided a new perspective about addictive behavior?

The Brain is pliable and Brain function can change

**?** | Why is developing empathy necessary to the healing process?

_____
_____
_____
_____
_____
_____
_____

**?** | What did you learn about your attachment style?

_____
_____
_____
_____
_____
_____
_____

**?** | How does our attachment style help us or hurt us in relationships?

_____
_____
_____
_____
_____
_____

**?** | How is learning about the ACEs Study helpful in connection with addictive behaviors?

_____
_____
_____
_____
_____
_____
_____
_____
_____
_____

**?** | Science suggests that sexual addiction is more than a moral issue—it's a brain issue. Why is this concept challenging for many people in the Church?

_____
_____
_____
_____
_____
_____
_____
_____
_____
_____
_____

# WEEKLY WORK

## ADVERSE CHILDHOOD EXPERIENCES (ACEs)[11]

**Prior to your 18th birthday:**

**01.** Did a parent or other adult in the household often or very often... Swear at you, insult you, put you down, or humiliate you? **OR** Act in a way that made you afraid that you might be physically hurt? .................................................... ☐ Yes ☐ No

**02.** Did a parent or other adult in the household often or very often... Push, grab, slap, or throw something at you? **OR** Ever hit you so hard that you had marks or were injured? .................................................... ☐ Yes ☐ No

**03.** Did an adult or person at least five years older than you ever... Touch or fondle you or have you touch their body in a sexual way? **OR** Attempt or actually have oral, anal, or vaginal intercourse with you? .................................................... ☐ Yes ☐ No

---

[11] Centers for Disease Control and Prevention. (2016, April 1). *Adverse Childhood Experiences (ACEs)*. Retrieved from http://www.cdc.gov/violenceprevention/acestudy/index.html

**04.** Did you often or very often feel that… No one in your family loved you or thought you were important or special? **OR** Your family didn't look out for each other, feel close to each other, or support each other? ⬝⬝⬝⬝⬝⬝⬝⬝⬝⬝⬝⬝⬝⬝⬝ ☐ Yes ☐ No

**05.** Did you often or very often feel that… You didn't have enough to eat, had to wear dirty clothes, and had no one to protect you? **OR** Your parents were too drunk or high to take care of you or take you to the doctor if you needed it?
⬝⬝⬝⬝⬝⬝⬝⬝⬝⬝⬝⬝⬝⬝⬝⬝⬝⬝⬝⬝⬝⬝⬝⬝⬝⬝⬝⬝ ☐ Yes ☐ No

**06.** Were your parents ever separated or divorced? ⬝⬝⬝⬝⬝⬝⬝⬝⬝⬝⬝⬝⬝ ☐ Yes ☐ No

**07.** Was your mother or stepmother: Often or very often pushed, grabbed, slapped, or had something thrown at her? **OR** Sometimes kicked, bitten, hit with a fist, or hit with something hard? **OR** Ever repeatedly hit over at least a few minutes or threatened with a gun or knife? ⬝⬝⬝⬝⬝⬝⬝⬝⬝⬝⬝⬝⬝ ☐ Yes ☐ No

**08.** Did you live with anyone who was a problem drinker or alcoholic, or who used street drugs? ⬝⬝⬝⬝⬝⬝⬝⬝⬝⬝⬝⬝⬝⬝⬝⬝⬝⬝⬝⬝ ☐ Yes ☐ No

**09.** Was a household member depressed or mentally ill, or did a household member attempt suicide? ⬝⬝⬝⬝⬝⬝⬝⬝⬝⬝⬝⬝⬝⬝⬝⬝ ☐ Yes ☐ No

**10.** Did a household member go to prison? ⬝⬝⬝⬝⬝⬝⬝⬝⬝⬝⬝⬝⬝ ☐ Yes ☐ No

**Now add up your "Yes" answers: This is your ACEs Score.** ⬝⬝⬝⬝⬝⬝⬝⬝⬝⬝⬝⬝⬝

If you scored one or more, you're in the majority. Two-thirds of the 17,000 participants in the original ACEs Study scored one or more. Of those, 87 percent scored higher than one. What does your score indicate? If you scored four or more Adverse Childhood Experiences, your early life experiences may have a lasting effect on your health, behaviors, and life potential as an adult.

# YOUR ADULT ATTACHMENT STYLE

When completing this questionnaire, please focus on one significant relationship—ideally a current or past partner as the focus here is on adult relationships. This does not necessarily need to be a romantic relationship but must be the individual with whom you feel the most connected. Who is your primary "go to" person if you're sick, in trouble, want to celebrate, call with news, etc.? This questionnaire is designed to be an interactive learning tool. Please highlight, circle, or comment on any statements that are particularly relevant to you or that you'd like to revisit for exploration at a later time. When responding, consider how strongly you identify with each statement. Using the scale below, respond in the space provided.

**Please understand that this is not meant to be a diagnostic tool**, but it's a good starting point to begin your personal exploration into your attachment styles.

---

**0** = Disagree  |  **1** = Sometimes Agree  |  **2** = Mostly Agree  |  **3** = Strongly Agree

---

## SECURE

**01.** I feel relaxed with my partner most of the time. ⋯⋯⋯⋯⋯⋯⋯⋯⋯ 0 1 2 ③

**02.** I find it easy to flow between being close and connected with my partner to being on my own. ⋯⋯⋯⋯⋯⋯⋯⋯⋯ 0 1 2 ③

**03.** If my partner and I hit a glitch, it is relatively easy for me to apologize, brainstorm a win-win solution, or repair the misattunement or disharmony. ⋯⋯⋯ 0 1 2 ③

**04.** People are essentially good at heart. ⋯⋯⋯⋯⋯⋯⋯⋯⋯ 0 1 ② 3

**05.** It is a priority to keep agreements with my partner. ⋯⋯⋯⋯⋯⋯ 0 1 2 ③

**06.** I attempt to discover and meet the needs of my partner whenever possible and I feel comfortable expressing my own needs. ⋯⋯⋯⋯⋯⋯ 0 1 2 ③

**07.** I actively protect my partner from others and from harm and attempt to maintain safety in our relationship. ⋯⋯⋯⋯⋯⋯ 0 1 2 ③

**08.** I look at my partner with kindness and caring and look forward to our time together. ⋯⋯⋯⋯⋯⋯ 0 1 2 ③

**09.** I am comfortable being affectionate with my partner. ⋯⋯⋯⋯⋯ 0 1 2 ③

**10.** I can keep secrets, protect my partner's privacy, and respect boundaries.
⋯⋯⋯⋯⋯⋯⋯⋯⋯⋯⋯⋯⋯⋯⋯⋯⋯⋯⋯⋯⋯⋯⋯⋯⋯⋯⋯⋯⋯⋯ 0 1 2 ③

**Section Total** ⋯⋯⋯⋯⋯⋯⋯⋯⋯⋯⋯⋯⋯⋯⋯⋯⋯⋯⋯⋯⋯ 29

# AVOIDANT/DISMISSIVE

**01.** When my partner arrives home or approaches me, I feel inexplicably stressed especially when he or she wants to connect. ⋯⋯⋯⋯⋯ ⓪ 1 2 3

**02.** I find myself minimizing the importance of close relationships in my life.
⋯⋯⋯⋯⋯⋯⋯⋯⋯⋯⋯⋯⋯⋯⋯⋯⋯⋯⋯⋯⋯⋯⋯⋯⋯⋯⋯⋯⋯⋯ 0 ① 2 3

**03.** I insist on self-reliance; I have difficulty reaching out when I need help, and I do many of life's tasks or my hobbies, alone. ⋯⋯⋯⋯⋯⋯ 0 1 ② 3

**04.** I sometimes feel superior in not needing others and wish others were more self-sufficient. ⋯⋯⋯⋯⋯⋯⋯⋯⋯⋯⋯⋯⋯⋯⋯⋯⋯ 0 1 ② 3

**05.** I feel like my partner is always there but would often prefer to have my own space unless I invite the connection. ⋯⋯⋯⋯⋯⋯⋯⋯ ⓪ 1 2 3

**06.** Sometimes I prefer casual sex instead of a committed relationship. ⋯⋯ ⓪ 1 2 3

**07.** I usually prefer relationships with things or animals instead of people. ⋯ ⓪ 1 2 3

**08.** I often find eye contact uncomfortable and particularly difficult to maintain.
⋯⋯⋯⋯⋯⋯⋯⋯⋯⋯⋯⋯⋯⋯⋯⋯⋯⋯⋯⋯⋯⋯⋯⋯⋯⋯⋯⋯⋯⋯ ⓪ 1 2 3

**09.** It is easier for me to think things through than to express myself emotionally.
⋯⋯⋯⋯⋯⋯⋯⋯⋯⋯⋯⋯⋯⋯⋯⋯⋯⋯⋯⋯⋯⋯⋯⋯⋯⋯⋯⋯⋯⋯ 0 ① 2 3

**10.** When I lose a relationship, at first I might experience separation elation and then become depressed. ⋯⋯⋯⋯⋯⋯⋯⋯⋯⋯⋯⋯⋯⋯ ⓪ 1 2 3

**Section Total** ⋯⋯⋯⋯⋯⋯⋯⋯⋯⋯⋯⋯⋯⋯⋯⋯⋯⋯⋯⋯⋯ 6

# ANXIOUS/AMBIVALENT

**01.** I am always yearning for something or someone that I feel I cannot have and rarely feeling satisfied. ⬤0 1 2 3

**02.** Sometimes, I over-function, over-adapt, over-accommodate others, or over-apologize for things I didn't do, in an attempt to stabilize connection. 0 ①1 2 3

**03.** Over-focusing on others, I tend to lose myself in relationships. ⬤0 1 2 3

**04.** It is difficult for me to say NO or to set realistic boundaries. 0 ①1 2 3

**05.** I chronically second-guess myself and sometimes wish I had said something differently. ⬤0 1 2 3

**06.** When I give more than I get, I often resent this and harbor a grudge. It is often difficult to receive love from my partner when they express it. ⬤0 1 2 3

**07.** It is difficult for me to be alone. If alone, I feel stressed, abandoned, hurt, and/or angry. 0 1 2 3

**08.** At the same time as I feel a deep wish to be close to my partner, I also have a paralyzing fear of losing the relationship. ⬤0 1 2 3

**09.** I want to be close with my partner, but feel angry at my partner at the same time. ⬤0 1 2 3

**10.** After anxiously awaiting my partner's arrival, I end up picking fights. ⬤0 1 2 3

**11.** I often tend to "merge" or lose myself in my partner and feel what they feel, or want what they want. ⬤0 1 2 3

**Section Total** 2

# DISORGANIZED/DISORIENTED

**01.** When I reach a certain level of intimacy with my partner, I sometimes experience inexplicable fear. ⬤0 1 2 3

**02.** When presented with problems, I often feel stumped and feel they are irresolvable. ⬤0 1 2 3

**03.** I have an exaggerated startle response when others approach me unexpectedly. ⟨0⟩ 1 2 3

**04.** My partner often comments or complains that I am controlling. ⟨0⟩ 1 2 3

**05.** I often expect the worst to happen in my relationship. ⟨0⟩ 1 2 3

**06.** Protection often feels out of reach. I struggle to feel safe with my partner. ⟨0⟩ 1 2 3

**07.** I have a hard time remembering and discussing the feelings related to my past attachment situations. I disconnect, dissociate, or get confused. ⟨0⟩ 1 2 3

**08.** Stuck in approach-avoidance patterns with my partner, I want closeness but am also afraid of the one I desire to be close with. ⟨0⟩ 1 2 3

**09.** My instinctive, active self-protective responses are often unavailable when possible danger is present—leaving me feeling immobilized, disconnected, or "gone." ⟨0⟩ 1 2 3

**10.** Because I am easily confused or disoriented, especially when stressed, it is important for my partner to keep arrangements simple and clear. ⟨0⟩ 1 2 3

**Section Total** ⟨0⟩

# SCORING

For each section, add up your responses and record your total number. The section with the highest number will likely correspond to your unique attachment style. You may discover a dominant style or mix of styles.

This questionnaire is not meant to be a label or diagnosis. It is only intended to indicate tendencies and prompt more useful, precise personal exploration.[12]

[12] © 2014 Diane Poole Heller, Ph.D. | 743 Club Circle Louisville, CO 80027 | (303) 586-1772
info@dianepooleheller.com | www.dianepooleheller.com

# Session 04.

# THE ADDICTED BRAIN

In the last session, we learned about the brain: how our behaviors and experiences create neural pathways in our brain. We also learned about the power of dopamine and how it contributes to our behavior, even our unwanted sexual behavior. How do we fix this? How do we start the process of renewing our mind?

In this session, we're going to learn more about the brain and how God created it for renewal. In a very practical way, we will learn how to put behaviors in place that will create new, healthy neural pathways in our brain and create new, healthy habits.

Too often, when we struggle with sexually compulsive and addictive behaviors, we're told to pray more or try harder. For many of us, this is not going to bring lifelong healing.

Lasting healing comes from understanding the brain and how it contributes to our behaviors; and also recognizing that we need the Holy Spirit to be active in our healing process.

# BRAIN SCIENCE

Historically, scientists thought our brain was fixed:[1] the brain we were born with was what we had to work with our entire lives. In recent years, scientists discovered that brain development was not only based on our biology, but the things happening to us and around us also contributed to our brain development.[2] Today, scientists recognize that our brain is not fixed, but capable of great change.

| EPIGENETICS | the study of changes in organisms caused by modification of gene expression rather than alteration of the genetic code itself. |
|---|---|

## DEPENDING ON OUR AGE, OUR BRAIN IS:

- ◉ Creating new neurons
- ◉ Developing new neurological connections and pathways
- ◉ Pruning excess neurons
- ◉ Changing its chemistry
- ◉ Reorganizing itself

> *Great is his faithfulness;*
> *his mercies begin afresh each morning.*
>
> **LAMENTATIONS 3:23 NLT**

| NEUROGENESIS | the process by which new neurons are generated in the brain. |
|---|---|

---

[1] Doidge, N. (2007). *The Brain That Changes Itself: Stories of Personal Triumph from the Frontiers of Brain Science.* New York, NY: Penguin Books. xv.

[2] Jennings, T. (2015). Brains, Addiction, and Conversion. The AACC. Retrieved from https://www.aacc.net/2016/08/30/brains-addiction-and-conversion-2/.

# "OUR BRAIN IS CHANGING MOMENT BY MOMENT AS WE ARE THINKING. BY OUR THINKING AND CHOOSING WE ARE REDESIGNING THE LANDSCAPE OF OUR BRAINS."[3]

**Here are a few examples of how our brain is capable of great change:**

## EXERCISE

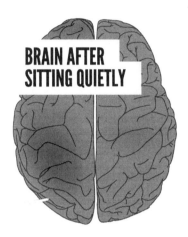
BRAIN AFTER SITTING QUIETLY

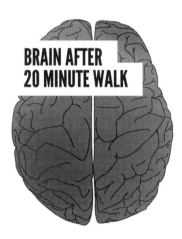
BRAIN AFTER 20 MINUTE WALK

Dr. Hillman and his colleagues conducted a study to determine whether exercise would increase academic performance.[4]

They had two comparisons: students sitting quietly for 20 minutes prior to taking an exam and students walking on a treadmill for 20 minutes prior to taking an exam.

Not only did imaging reveal much more neural activity in the brain when the students walked on the treadmill for 20 minutes prior to taking the exam, but the students increased their exam score by more than a letter grade.

---

[3] Leaf, C. (2013). *Switch on Your Brain: The Key to Peak Happiness, Thinking, and Health*. Grand Rapids, MI: Baker Publishing Group.

[4] Donnelly, J. E., Hillman, C. H., Castelli, D., Etnier, J. L., Lee, S., Tomporowski, P., Lambourne, K., & Szabo-Reed, A. N. (2016). Physical Activity, Fitness, Cognitive Function, and Academic Achievement in Children: A Systematic Review. *Medicine and science in sports and exercise, 48*(6), 1197–1222. https://doi.org/10.1249/MSS.0000000000000901

# NEUROPLASTICITY

| NEUROPLASTICITY | the brain's ability to reorganize itself by forming new neural connections. |

Neuroplasticity allows neurons in the brain to compensate for injury and adjust their activities in response to what is happening in the brain—when it recognizes that change is needed.[5]

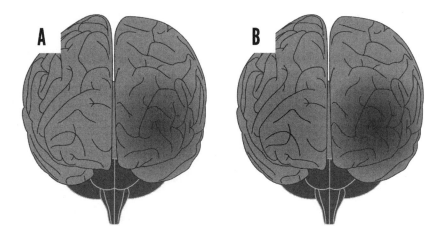

**Image A:** this person has experienced some form of brain damage to their left prefrontal cortex.

**Image B:** the right prefrontal cortex recognized that change was needed, compensating and reorganizing itself to be more efficient.

New neural connection forms at a rapid rate when we are intentional about putting new behaviors and tools in place to strengthen our brain.

Our brain wants to be healthy. When we are willing to do the hard work—the work of renewing our mind—our brain will find a way.

_____

_____

_____

_____

_____

[5] Doidge, N. (2007). *The Brain That Changes Itself: Stories of Personal Triumph from the Frontiers of Brain Science*. New York, NY: Penguin Books. 254.

**?** | Why is breaking the Shame Cycle an important step
to the healing process?

_____

_____

_____

_____

_____

_____

_____

_____

_____

_____

_____

**?** | How does the Iceberg Illustration support how we get trapped in unhealthy
behavior patterns? How does it support the process of finding healing?

_____

_____

_____

_____

_____

_____

_____

_____

_____

_____

_____

> **THE VERY STRUCTURE OF OUR BRAIN—THE RELATIVE SIZE OF DIFFERENT REGIONS, THE STRENGTH OF CONNECTIONS BETWEEN THEM, EVEN THEIR FUNCTIONS—REFLECTS THE LIVES WE HAVE LED. LIKE SAND ON A BEACH, THE BRAIN BEARS THE FOOTPRINTS OF THE DECISIONS WE HAVE MADE, THE SKILLS WE HAVE LEARNED, AND THE ACTIONS WE HAVE TAKEN.[6]**

[6] Bagley, S. (2007). *The Brain: How The Brain Rewires Itself*. Time Magazine. January 19.

# THE MAKING OF A SEX ADDICT

Research conducted by Dr. Patrick Carnes reveals common characteristics among people who struggle with unwanted sexual behaviors.[7] A more exhaustive list of results can be found on pages 150-151.

## FAMILY

- Addicts in Family **87%**
- Rigid Family System **77%**
- Disengaged Family System **87%**
- Rigid/Disengaged Family System **68%**

## ABUSE/EARLY TRAUMA

- Emotional **97%**
- Sexual **81%**
- Physical **72%**

## OTHER ADDICTIONS

- Chemical Dependency **42%**
- Eating Disorders **38%**
- Compulsive Working **28%**
- Compulsive Spending **26%**
- Compulsive Gambling **5%**

For many men and women who struggle with sexually compulsive and addictive behaviors, it's typically not one isolated experience that pulled them into their unhealthy behaviors. More likely, it was dozens, if not hundreds, of experiences happening to them and around them that created the perfect storm.

---

[7] Carnes, P. (2004). The Making of a Sex Addict. Revised and updated version of "The Obsessive Shadow" (1998). IITAP. Retrieved from https://cdn.ymaws.com/iitap.com/resource/resmgr/arie_files/m1_article_the-making-of-a-s.pdf

# ONE BRAIN GENERATES MORE ELECTRICAL IMPULSES IN ONE DAY THAN ALL THE CELL PHONES ON THE PLANET.[8]

_____

_____

_____

_____

_____

_____

_____

_____

# DEVELOPING MENTAL TOUGHNESS[9]

Implementing these tools into our daily lives will be foundational to our healing process. These four practices are used in Pure Desire materials.

## GOAL SETTING

Three basic rules for goal setting:

**01.** Only set three goals for yourself at a time.

**02.** Focus on short term goals.

**03.** Create positive goals.

---

[8] Leaf, C. (2013). _Switch on Your Brain: The Key to Peak Happiness, Thinking, and Health._ Grand Rapids, MI: Baker Publishing Group.

[9] Lambertsen, C. (2016). _Navy SEALs Mental Toughness: A Guide To Developing An Unbeatable Mind._ Scotts Valley, CA: CreateSpace.

# MENTAL REHEARSAL

The process of imagining ourselves doing something—especially something fearful or stressful—can actually help us to be more successful.

## YOUR BRAIN DOESN'T KNOW THE DIFFERENCE BETWEEN IMAGINING YOURSELF DOING SOMETHING YOU HAVE TO DO AND ACTUALLY DOING IT.

Developing an attitude of gratitude often goes hand-in-hand with practicing mental rehearsal.

**GRATITUDE**     having a distinct awareness of the goodness in our lives.

Writing down the things we are grateful for, even when we don't feel grateful, can help us practice an attitude of gratitude.

_____

_____

_____

_____

_____

_____

_____

_____

_____

_____

# POSITIVE SELF-TALK

We talk to ourselves approximately 300-1,000 words per minute. That's at least four times faster than we can talk out loud.

Think about this: if we woke up in a negative mindset, in about five minutes, we could speak almost 4,000 negative words to ourselves.

We must identify where our negative messages come from—the lies that live in our limbic system that keep us in isolation, that keep us from relationship with God and others.

There's another saying in neuroscience that supports this process of renewing the mind:

## NEURONS OUT OF SYNC FAIL TO LINK.[10]

The more we stop our unhealthy behaviors and put new behaviors in place, the old neurological pathways in our brain are going to fade away and lose the power they had over us.

We cannot create positive self-talk while we are stuck in a negative core belief. This is why we need a group; a safe healthy community to speak truth into our lives.

_____
_____
_____
_____
_____
_____
_____
_____
_____
_____

[10] Doidge, N. (2007). *The Brain That Changes Itself: Stories of Personal Triumph from the Frontiers of Brain Science.* New York, NY: Penguin Books. 64.

# AROUSAL CONTROL

| **AROUSAL** | to evoke or awaken a feeling, emotion, or response. Arousal is often related to a person's perception and/or intensity of an event, which can either fuel or inhibit action. |
|---|---|

Arousal control is so important to the healing process because for many of us who struggle with addictive behaviors, it was the stresses of life that influenced our unhealthy behaviors.

Many forms of meditation focus on clearing our mind. However, biblical meditation focuses on filling our mind with attributes of God and His word.

> ## SOCIAL MEDIA INTERFERES WITH CLEAR THINKING AND DECISION MAKING, A LACK OF SELF-CONTROL, AND IMPULSIVE BEHAVIORS.[11]

> ## GREATER SOCIAL MEDIA USE IS ASSOCIATED WITH A HIGHER BODY MASS INDEX, INCREASED BINGE EATING, A LOWER CREDIT SCORE, AND HIGHER LEVELS OF CREDIT CARD DEBT.

In our technological world, being able to calm our minds is so important. Technology and social media are not evil; they are a reality of our world. For many of us who struggle with addictive behaviors, developing healthy online behaviors will be an essential part of our healing process.

---

11 Wilcox, K., & Stephen, A. T. (2013). Are close friends the enemy? Online social networks, self-esteem, and self-control. *Journal of Consumer Research, 40*(1), 90–103.

# COGNITIVE BEHAVIORAL THERAPY[12]

Cognitive Behavior Therapy focuses not only on our current behaviors, but looks at how our past pain and trauma are contributing to our current behaviors. It takes into consideration the origin of our maladaptive behaviors—where our behaviors come from—to help us understand why we do what we do.

> ## LISTENING TO OUR LUST HAS SO MUCH TO TEACH US IF WE'RE WILLING TO PAY ATTENTION.
>
> **JAY STRINGER**

_____

_____

_____

_____

_____

_____

_____

We have to risk going back into the mess and darkness so that we can change our future behavior.

## PRACTICE DOESN'T MAKE PERFECT; PRACTICE MAKES PERMANENT.[13]

---

[12] Rosenberg, K. & Feder, L. (2014). _Behavioral Addictions: Criteria, Evidence, and Treatment._ London, UK: Elsevier, Inc. 13.

[13] Vince Lombardi Quotes. (n.d.). BrainyQuote.com. Retrieved from https://www.brainyquote.com/quotes/vince_lombardi_138158

# Session 04.

# REFLECTION QUESTIONS

**?** | How does learning about renewing the mind encourage us to begin the healing process? (For ourselves or as an encouragement to someone we love?)

_____

_____

_____

_____

_____

**?** | Why is developing mental toughness an essential piece to our overall health?

_____

_____

_____

_____

_____

**?** Which element of developing mental toughness do you struggle with (goal setting, mental rehearsal, positive self-talk, arousal control)? Why?

_____

_____

_____

_____

_____

_____

_____

**?** If we know that our brain is capable of great change and we have tools to help us in our healing, what are some of the realistic obstacles we face?

_____

_____

_____

_____

_____

_____

**?** What are some ways you can battle negative self-talk?

_____

_____

_____

_____

_____

_____

_____

_____

**?** | Why is being part of a safe group important for our healing?

_____

_____

_____

_____

_____

_____

_____

_____

_____

_____

**?** | Last week, you were asked to complete the ACE Evaluation. What was most insightful about completing the evaluation?

_____

_____

_____

_____

_____

_____

_____

_____

_____

_____

# Session 04.

# WEEKLY WORK

## GRATITUDE JOURNAL

Each day this week, write down one thing for which you are grateful. Fill in the days of the week as they align with your group meeting.

**DAY**                      **I AM GRATEFUL FOR...**

# MENTAL TOUGHNESS EXERCISE

Select one area of mental toughness to practice this week: goal setting, mental rehearsal, positive self-talk, or arousal control (breathing and meditation). Practice throughout the week, keeping track of how you feel when you're done.

| TASK | I FELT... |
|------|-----------|
| *Example: Positive self-talk* | *silly at first, but the more I practiced, the more confident I felt.* |
| | |
| | |
| | |
| | |
| | |
| | |

**Journal your experience.**

# Session 05.

# TOOLS FOR SOBRIETY

In our current culture, we are continually bombarded with sexual content in ads, movies, social media, and more. When it comes to living in sexual health, how do we make sense of our past pain and negative sexual experiences so that we can live a life of sexual integrity?

In this session, we will talk through foundational tools that are essential for living in freedom. If we can make sense of our past experiences it will help us create a roadmap toward sexual health.

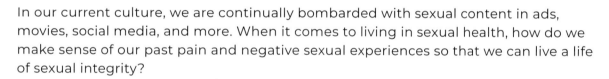

IN ORDER TO TURN FROM UNWANTED SEXUAL BEHAVIOR, AN INDIVIDUAL MUST UNDERSTAND WHERE TO CHANGE THEIR THINKING ABOUT SEX AND SEXUALITY.

Our thinking has been deeply impacted by the world around us.

_____

_____

_____

_____

_____

_____

As we look at sexual health and healing, and wanting to be people who live in a new way, we all start in a similar place. We're being invited to live in a new kingdom, perhaps much different than the kingdom in which we grew up.

To find lasting healing, we have to be willing to turn from our culture and the kingdom where we've been living.

_____

_____

_____

_____

_____

_____

_____

# CHANGING OUR THINKING

In order to turn from sexual behavior, an individual must understand where to change their thinking about sex and sexuality.

It's not enough to be culturally aware of how we've been conditioned sexually. We have to look specifically at what's happened in our story and in our lives.

_____

_____

_____

# THE AROUSAL TEMPLATE

**AROUSAL** where the brain is reacting to all kinds of stimuli that trigger an individual to a heightened state of awareness.

Arousal might be caused by something fearful or exciting, or even something sexual.

## AROUSAL IS AMORAL.

Arousal is a combination of how our body is designed to respond—what's natural, how our DNA responds, and the way the human brain is designed—but also a byproduct of our experiences and upbringing.

Arousal is a subconscious response. It's tied to our survival instincts—a limbic system response. Our sexuality is tied to our limbic system because **our brain views food and sex as part of the survival system**.

Remember: "**Neurons that fire together, wire together.**" This is true, whether the experience is good or bad.

This is why almost anything can become a trigger for sexual arousal: sights, smells, locations, objects and feelings, such as pain, fear, anger, shame, joy and boredom could all become part of creating arousal in our lives.

> ## OUR PURSUIT OF UNWANTED SEXUAL BEHAVIOR IS SHAPED AND PREDICTED BY THE PARTS OF OUR STORIES THAT WERE NEVER ADDRESSED.
>
> JAY STRINGER

> ## RATHER THAN TRYING TO STOP OUR UNWANTED SEXUAL BEHAVIORS WE NEED TO CONSIDER THAT OUR UNWANTED SEXUAL BEHAVIOR ACTUALLY CONTAINS THE KEYS TO THE FREEDOM THAT WE'RE SEEKING.
>
> JAY STRINGER

> ## WHAT AROUSES US IS NOT AN INDICATOR OF OUR CHARACTER, BUT OF OUR HISTORY AND OF OUR LEARNING FROM THOSE EXPERIENCES.

If we can recognize our arousal pattern and see where it's coming from, then we can understand our story. When we understand our story, we can partner with the Holy Spirit, and others in our life, to change its power over us.

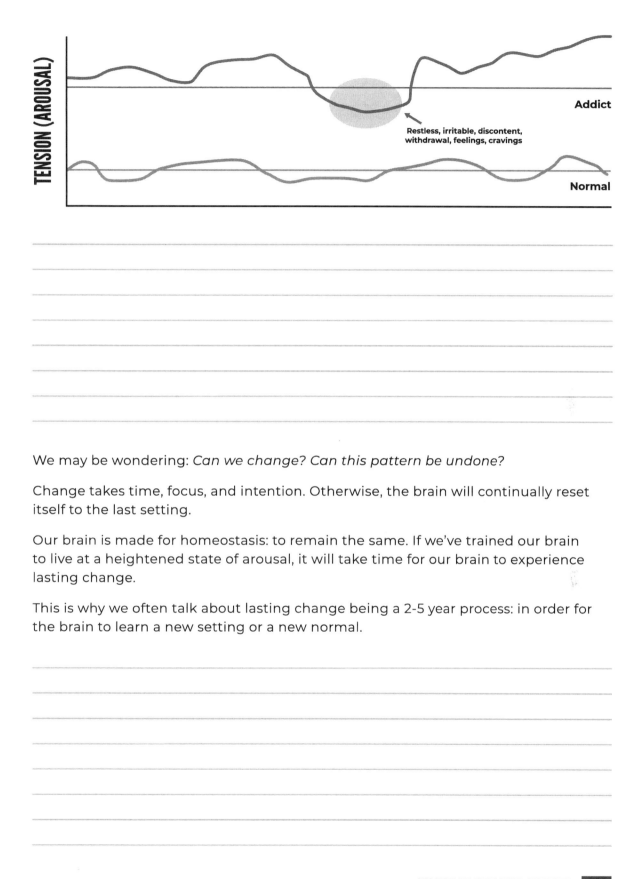

**TENSION (AROUSAL)**

Addict

Restless, irritable, discontent, withdrawal, feelings, cravings

Normal

We may be wondering: *Can we change? Can this pattern be undone?*

Change takes time, focus, and intention. Otherwise, the brain will continually reset itself to the last setting.

Our brain is made for homeostasis: to remain the same. If we've trained our brain to live at a heightened state of arousal, it will take time for our brain to experience lasting change.

This is why we often talk about lasting change being a 2-5 year process: in order for the brain to learn a new setting or a new normal.

# THE AROUSAL TEMPLATE:
# APPLICATION

The Arousal Template is a great tool for helping us identify arousal in our lives and what's created this template for us. Whether we struggle with unwanted sexual behaviors or not, each of us has an arousal template.

It's important to work vertically through the steps, not horizontally.

**Step 01:** Make a list of every trigger or problematic behavior.

**Step 02:** Make a list of every painful sexual or relational experience early in life.

**Step 03:** Make a list of what you remember thinking and feeling about the experiences listed in step 2.

**Step 04:** Make a list of current core beliefs or overall themes you're finding problematic.

**Step 05:** In light of the first four steps, what patterns emerge?

We want to make sure these practical steps are not pulled from the air or random ideas, but are linked to what we've experienced.

| Step 01: The specific triggers and behaviors for me | Step 02: Early painful sexual relational experiences | Step 03: As a child, how did you feel and act? | Step 04: Your overall themes and core beliefs | Step 05: Relapse patterns, triggers, and recovery strategies |
|---|---|---|---|---|
| *Pornography* | *Parents' divorce: fighting over kids* | *Relationships are expendable.* | *I'm not lovable.* | **Inner Circle** |
| *Masturbating* | *Disconnected family* | *I was not valued, because I couldn't follow the rules as well as my siblings.* | *I'm invisible, even to those who are supposed to love me.* | |
| *R-rated movies* | *All rules, no relationship* | | | |
| *Sexually-explicit TV* | *Dad said, "Quit your crying and grow up."* | *I avoided feeling emotions.* | *I'm a survivor. I can figure out life on my own.* | |
| *Fantasizing* | | | | **Middle Circle** |
| *Foul language* | *Break-up one week before prom* | *Don't let loved ones get too close.* | *Real relationships are overrated.* | |
| *Explicit novels and magazines* | *Found explicit magazine in dad's closet* | *Don't count on anyone.* | | |
| *Browsing online video or app stores* | *Ridiculed for my weight* | *Sexual fantasy is an escape.* | | |
| *Isolating/ Avoiding family and friends* | *Discovered masturbation; never talked about at home* | *I'm not cool enough for a boyfriend/ girlfriend.* | | **Outer Circle** |
| *Sarcasm* | | | | |
| *Out of town on business* | *Sexually abused by uncle* | *My body type is the most important thing.* | | |
| *Home alone* | | | | |
| *Malls* | | | | |
| *Chat rooms* | | | | |

# THE RELAPSE PREVENTION TOOL

## THREE CIRCLES TOOL | an individual game plan for sexual health.

## 01. DEFINE SOBRIETY: THE CRASH.

List all the behaviors we are addicted to or we're committed to stopping. This is our Inner Circle. In order to remain in sobriety, or in health, we must abstain from these behaviors.

## 02. DETERMINE GUARDRAILS.

List all the things we choose not to do because they can lead to the Inner Circle or acting out. This is our Middle Circle. Guardrails keep us healthy.

### WE'LL NEVER REGRET A WALL TOO HIGH, THAT WAS DIFFICULT TO GET OVER; BUT WE WILL ALWAYS REGRET A WALL TOO LOW, THAT WAS EASY TO STEP OVER.

The same is true when determining guardrails in our lives.

## 03. DEVELOPING HEALTH.

List all the things that bring joy, contentment, peace of mind, and fulfillment—this is what developing health is all about. This is our Outer Circle. The behaviors in our Outer Circle actually change our neurochemistry and help us deal with cravings and stress. These are behaviors that represent self-care.

# ADDITIONAL TIPS

**01.** The items in The Three Circles tool are not fixed. Over time, we may recognize how a behavior in our Middle Circle needs to move to our Inner Circle. As we move toward health, some behaviors may be no longer necessary and are removed from our Three Circles.

**02.** Our goal is not behavior modification; it's overall health.

**03.** Completing the Arousal Template and Relapse Prevention Tool (The Three Circles) alone will have limited success. As we engage in our healing with others, we will have more success in building a game plan for long-term health.

OUTER CIRCLE

MIDDLE CIRCLE

**HEALTH**

**GUARDRAILS**

**DEFINE SOBRIETY**

pornography
masturbation
flirting at work

having a plan when traveling
not surfing internet alone
not watching tv alone at night

making weekly phone calls to group, telling my spouse about my day
exercising regularly, getting 7 hours of sleep a night

# Session 05.

# REFLECTION QUESTIONS

**?** | How have we been culturally conditioned to think about sex and sexuality?

_____

_____

_____

_____

**?** | Why do we struggle with changing our thinking about sex and sexuality? What obstacles do we face?

_____

_____

_____

_____

_____

**?** In creating a game plan for health, why is it important that we evaluate our past painful sexual and relational experiences?

**?** Which of the 5 steps in the Arousal Template seems most challenging to identify?

**?** When we struggle with unwanted behavior, we too often focus on those negative behaviors and how to avoid them. But what are some ways we can pursue healthy habits (outer circle)?

_____
_____
_____
_____
_____
_____
_____
_____
_____
_____
_____

**?** Last week, how successful were you at developing mental toughness? What mental toughness tool did you choose to implement and how did it work?

_____
_____
_____
_____
_____
_____
_____
_____
_____
_____
_____
_____

# WEEKLY WORK

## AROUSAL TEMPLATE

| Step 01: The specific triggers and behaviors for me | Step 02: Early painful sexual relational experiences | Step 03: As a child, how did you feel and act? | Step 04: Your overall themes and core beliefs | Step 05: Arousal patterns, triggers, and recovery strategies |
|---|---|---|---|---|
| | | | | **Inner Circle** |
| | | | | **Middle Circle** |
| | | | | **Outer Circle** |

# THREE CIRCLES TOOL

HEALTH

GUARDRAILS

DEFINE
SOBRIETY

# Session 06.

# THE NEED FOR COMMUNITY

Many men and women who struggle with unwanted sexual behaviors or who have experienced betrayal live in isolation. They feel alone and fear the exposure of others finding out their secret. What they need is a safe, confidential community to start their healing.

In this session, we'll discover why a group setting is essential when it comes to lasting healing. We'll walk through several foundational tools used in Pure Desire group materials and how they contribute to recovery for the addict and support for the betrayed.

When we're talking about sexual addiction recovery, we need community.

> *Two are better than one, because they have a good return for their labor:*
>
> *If either of them falls down, one can help the other up. But pity anyone who falls and has no one to help them up. Also, if two lie down together, they will keep warm. But how can one keep warm alone? Though one may be overpowered, two can defend themselves. A cord of three strands is not quickly broken.*

## ECCLESIASTES 4:9-12

We can only take in so much information and our brain can only process what we're focused on. This is why we need others in our lives—those who have been there before us—to point out what we've missed, especially when going through tough stuff.

# ONE PERSON'S STORY

Marriage doesn't fix things; it only reveals more of what's there.

Many people in the Church are struggling with sexually compulsive behaviors. They carry a deep dark secret and feel that they cannot be fully vulnerable.

Our churches are full of hurting men and women, who have secrets, and most churches don't have a program or any way to help. For many, it feels hopeless.

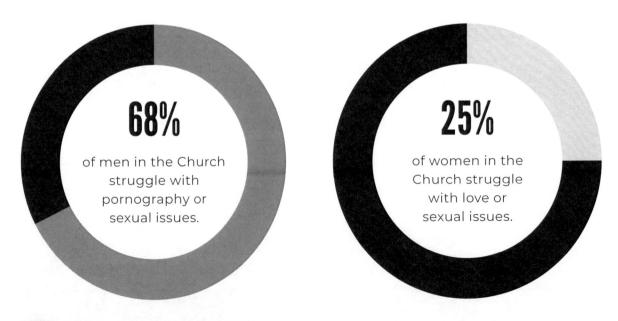

**68%** of men in the Church struggle with pornography or sexual issues.

**25%** of women in the Church struggle with love or sexual issues.

**LOVE ADDICTION**

The reliance on someone else for validation. This may include attempting to get unmet needs fulfilled, avoiding fear or emotional pain, reenacting past trauma in an effort to solve problems and maintain balance. In an attempt to gain control of our lives, we become out of control by giving personal power to someone or something else, resulting in unhealthy dependency on others, romantic illusions, or sex.

**SEX ADDICTION**

A compulsive behavior of an individual who cannot manage their sexual thoughts and actions despite repeated attempts to stop the behaviors and the potential for devastating negative consequences.

# GROUP RESOURCES

## FOR THOSE WHO STRUGGLE

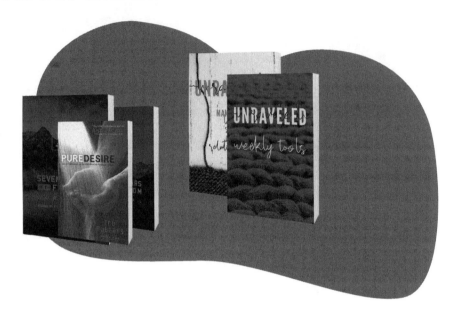

We have group resources for men and women who struggle with unwanted sexual behaviors.

When we're in a group, it is a safe place where we process little bits of information at a time, one layer at a time.

When we verbally process our life story out loud, it lights up many different areas of the brain. It taps into our memories and emotions, stored together in our brain, and helps to neutralize some of the feelings attached to the memories. As we process out loud in a safe community, our painful memories and triggers will start to calm down. This deep healing happens when we heal with others.

_____

_____

_____

_____

_____

_____

_____

# FOR THOSE BETRAYED

We have group resources for men and women who have experienced betrayal. This provides very practical steps for healing. Whether we know about our spouse's addiction or not, living with an addict is living with trauma and this affects our behaviors.

# FOR TEENS/YOUNG ADULTS WHO STRUGGLE

We have group resources for teens/young adults: boys and girls. As parents, when we pursue healing, sexual health becomes part of our language. It's not about sitting down with our kids and having one conversation about sex and sexuality. It's about having an ongoing conversation about healthy sexuality.

For parents or youth leaders: we would have our own workbook and answer the questions from when we were a teenager. When sharing our answers, what we struggled with as a teen, this helps to lower shame. It helps teens recognize that their struggles are normal.

When we share our story, God uses the power of our testimony to give others hope.

# REFLECTION QUESTIONS

**?** | Why is being in community or in a recovery/support group important for the healing process?

_____

_____

_____

_____

_____

**?** | What thoughts come to mind when considering the amount of men and women struggling with sexual issues in the Church? How does it make you feel?

_____

_____

_____

_____

_____

_____

_____

**?** How aware are you of your emotional state at any given point during the week? Do you see ways that the FASTER Scale would improve your emotional awareness?

_____

_____

_____

_____

_____

_____

_____

_____

_____

_____

**?** What is a problem you face regularly and have a hard time changing? Can you identify what the double bind might be in this situation?

_____

_____

_____

_____

_____

_____

_____

_____

_____

_____

**?** Have you seen examples in life where small, incremental progress led to major changes or accomplishment? Share a few. How could making one primary commitment each week help someone make lasting change in their life?

_____

_____

_____

_____

_____

_____

_____

_____

_____

_____

**?** What challenges did you face when completing the Arousal Template and Three Circles exercises last week? How was it helpful?

_____

_____

_____

_____

_____

_____

_____

_____

_____

_____

# WEEKLY WORK

## FASTER SCALE

Adapted with permission from the *Genesis Process* by Michael Dye.

### PART ONE

**Check the behaviors on the FASTER Scale that you identify with in each section.**

**R** **estoration:** Accepting life on God's terms, with trust, grace, mercy, vulnerability and gratitude.

☐ No current secrets

☐ Working to resolve problems

☐ Identifying fears and feelings

☐ Keeping commitments to meetings, prayer, family, church, people, goals, and self

☐ Being open and honest

☐ Making eye contact

☐ Increasing in relationships with God and others

☐ True accountability

**F** **orgetting Priorities:** Start believing the present circumstances and moving away from trusting God.

- ☐ Denial
- ☐ Flight
- ☐ A change in what's important (how you spend your time, energy, & thoughts)
- ☐ Secrets
- ☐ Less time/energy for God, meetings, church
- ☐ Avoiding support and accountability people
- ☐ Superficial conversations
- ☐ Sarcasm
- ☐ Isolating
- ☐ Changes in goals

- ☐ Obsessed with relationships
- ☐ Breaking promises & commitments
- ☐ Neglecting family
- ☐ Preoccupation with material things, TV, computers, entertainment
- ☐ Procrastination
- ☐ Lying
- ☐ Overconfidence
- ☐ Bored
- ☐ Hiding money
- ☐ Image management
- ☐ Seeking to control situations and other people

*Forgetting priorities will lead to the inclusion of:*

**A** **nxiety:** A growing background noise of undefined fear; getting energy from emotions.

- ☐ Worry
- ☐ Using profanity
- ☐ Being fearful
- ☐ Being resentful
- ☐ Replaying old, negative thoughts
- ☐ Perfectionism
- ☐ Judging other's motives
- ☐ Making goals/lists you can't complete
- ☐ Mind reading

- ☐ Fantasy
- ☐ Codependent rescuing
- ☐ Sleep problems
- ☐ Trouble concentrating
- ☐ Seeking/creating drama
- ☐ Gossip
- ☐ Using over-the-counter medication for pain, sleep or weight control
- ☐ Flirting

*Anxiety then leads to the inclusion of:*

# S peeding Up: Trying to outrun the anxiety which is usually the first sign of depression.

- ☐ Super busy and always in a hurry (finding good reason to justify the work)
- ☐ Workaholic
- ☐ Can't relax
- ☐ Avoiding slowing down
- ☐ Feeling driven
- ☐ Can't turn off thoughts
- ☐ Skipping meals
- ☐ Binge eating (usually at night)
- ☐ Overspending
- ☐ Can't identify own feelings/needs
- ☐ Repetitive negative thoughts
- ☐ Irritable
- ☐ Dramatic mood swings
- ☐ Too much caffeine
- ☐ Over-exercising
- ☐ Nervousness
- ☐ Difficulty being alone/with people
- ☐ Difficulty listening to others
- ☐ Making excuses for having to "do it all"

*Speeding Up then leads to the inclusion of:*

# T icked Off: Getting adrenaline high on anger and aggression.

- ☐ Procrastination causing crisis in money, work, and relationships
- ☐ Increased sarcasm
- ☐ Black and white (all or nothing) thinking
- ☐ Feeling alone
- ☐ Nobody understands
- ☐ Overreacting
- ☐ Road rage
- ☐ Constant resentments
- ☐ Pushing others away
- ☐ Increasing isolation
- ☐ Blaming
- ☐ Arguing
- ☐ Irrational thinking
- ☐ Can't take criticism
- ☐ Defensive
- ☐ People avoiding you
- ☐ Needing to be right
- ☐ Digestive problems
- ☐ Headaches
- ☐ Obsessive (stuck) thoughts
- ☐ Can't forgive
- ☐ Feeling superior
- ☐ Using intimidation

*Ticked Off then leads to the inclusion of:*

# E xhausted: Loss of physical and emotional energy; coming off the adrenaline high, and the onset of depression.

☐ Depressed

☐ Panicked

☐ Confused

☐ Hopelessness

☐ Sleeping too much or too little

☐ Can't cope

☐ Overwhelmed

☐ Crying for "no reason"

☐ Can't think

☐ Forgetful

☐ Pessimistic

☐ Helpless

☐ Tired

☐ Numb

☐ Wanting to run

☐ Constant cravings for old coping behaviors

☐ Thinking of using sex, drugs, or alcohol

☐ Seeking old unhealthy people & places

☐ Really isolating

☐ People angry with you

☐ Self-abuse

☐ Suicidal thoughts

☐ Spontaneous crying

☐ No goals

☐ Survival mode

☐ Not returning phone calls

☐ Missing work

☐ Irritability

☐ No appetite

*Exhausted then leads to the inclusion of:*

# R elapse: Returning to the place you swore you would never go again. Coping with life on your terms. You sitting in the driver's seat instead of God.

☐ Giving up and giving in

☐ Out of control

☐ Lost in your addiction

☐ Lying to yourself and others

☐ Feeling you just can't manage without your coping behaviors, at least for now. The result is the reinforcement of shame, guilt and condemnation; and feelings of abandonment and being alone.

# PART TWO

**Identify the most powerful behavior in each section and write it next to the corresponding heading.**

**Answer the following three questions:**

**01.** How does it affect me? How do I feel in the moment?

**02.** How does it affect the important people in my life?

**03.** Why do I do this? What is the benefit for me?

### Restoration

**01.**

**02.**

**03.**

### Forgetting Priorities

**01.**

**02.**

**03.**

### Anxiety

**01.**

**02.**

**03.**

## Speeding Up

01. _____

_____

02. _____

_____

03. _____

_____

## Ticked Off

01. _____

_____

02. _____

_____

03. _____

_____

## Exhausted

01. _____

_____

02. _____

_____

03. _____

_____

## Relapse

01. _____

_____

02. _____

_____

03. _____

_____

Get more blank copies of the FASTER Scale at **puredesire.org/tools**.

# COMMITMENT TO CHANGE EXERCISE

**?** | **1.** What area do you need to change or what challenge are you facing next week?

**?** | **2.** What will it cost you emotionally if you do change? What fear will you have to face?

**?** | **3.** What will it cost you if you don't change?

**?** | **4.** What is your plan to maintain your restoration regarding these changes?

**?** | **5.** Who will keep you accountable to this commitment?

Name _____ Day _____

Name _____ Day _____

Name _____ Day _____

**?** | **6.** What are the details of your accountability for this week? What questions should they ask you?

# Session 07.

# RELATIONSHIPS & RECOVERY

When it comes to our sexual health, getting healthy doesn't just heal us. It has a way of spilling into all our relationships, bringing life and healing to those around us.

In this session, we'll dig a little deeper and uncover some of the relationship dynamics that take place when individuals, couples, and families start getting healthy together. We'll talk through several tools that give insight into common issues people face and how they learn to communicate their needs in a healthy way.

> ## WHEN WE DENY OUR STORIES, THEY DEFINE US. WHEN WE OWN OUR STORIES, WE GET TO WRITE A BRAVE NEW ENDING.[1]

_____

_____

_____

_____

[1] Brown, B. (2015). Own our history. Change the story [Blog post]. June 18. Retrieved from https://brenebrown.com/blog/2015/06/18/own-our-history-change-the-story/.

> ## SEXUAL DISCIPLESHIP IS INTEGRATING DISCIPLESHIP AND SEXUALITY IN A WAY THAT HELPS US BE PREPARED NOT JUST TO RESPOND BASED ON WHAT WE KNOW BUT RESPOND OUT OF OUR LIVES AND REALLY UNDERSTAND WHAT IT MEANS TO FOLLOW CHRIST WITH OUR SEXUALITY.
>
> JULI SLATTERY

# UNHEALTHY SEXUALITY VS. HEALTHY SEXUALITY

## UNHEALTHY SEXUALITY

- Degrades & shames
- Demanding & obligatory
- Victimizes & exploits
- Lacks emotional attachment
- Needs dominated by one
- Built on dishonesty
- Is unsafe, creating fear
- Serves to medicate pain
- Meets self-focused needs
- Compromises values & beliefs
- Reflects a double life

## HEALTHY SEXUALITY

- Respectful
- Fun & exciting
- Victimless
- Intimate
- Mutuality in needs expressed
- Trust is foundational
- Safe
- Serves to connect emotionally
- Creates warmth & oneness
- Deepens values & beliefs
- Authentic

Many people wonder: *What's okay and not okay when it comes to sex in marriage?*

The attitudes and behaviors listed in each column provide a great place to start.

When we are unable to vocalize our sexual feelings and needs, it can lead to unhealthy sexual and emotional experiences in marriage.

Whether we're married or single, this chart applies.

Single people who have never had sex may think they're sexually healthy. If they are using fantasy and masturbation, which is self-focused, these things will impact their future relationship.

How do we develop health sexuality? This starts with normalizing the conversation about sexual health. A great way to do this is by being in a group—processing our past pain and trauma with others. This is how we develop sexual health. It doesn't happen overnight.

Some married people may think, *I don't even like sex, so I don't need to be in a group.* Whether we're experiencing hypersexual behaviors (extreme sexual interest) or hyposexual behaviors (low to no sexual interest), it often comes from the same place--a place of trauma and sexual brokenness.

God intended for sex to be a mutually enjoyable experience between a husband and wife.

# DISCLOSURE

Disclosure can be a difficult subject and never easy. Whether we're the one confessing or the one who's been lied to, disclosure is an important part of the healing process.

## FULL DISCLOSURE

Full disclosure is when the struggling spouse/significant other provides a full, fact-based report of their sexual history. It is usually recommended after six months of sobriety has been established.

Pure Desire strongly suggests that disclosure is done with a Certified Sex Addiction Therapist (CSAT) or someone who has experience in this arena. Using a professional clinician is encouraged as they can walk and counsel a couple through the disclosure process effectively. This is the best way to minimize potential damage done through disclosure and ensure both spouses are supported.

## STAGGERED DISCLOSURE

Staggered disclosure is when the struggling spouse/significant other continues to disclose more information as they remember it. For the betrayed spouse/significant other, this feels like "death by a thousand cuts."

## FORCED DISCLOSURE

Forced disclosure is when negative sexual behavior has been discovered that includes illegal activities (e.g., sexual activity with minors) or requires immediate action. This leads to a forced disclosure. It is best to handle a forced disclosure with a CSAT or trained professional.

Full disclosure and being honest during the recovery process are not the same thing. Honesty and transparency are strongly encouraged in regards to relapses during recovery. The most effective time for a full disclosure is near the end of a Pure Desire group. This gives the person struggling the opportunity to write out a clear and complete narrative of their sexual history. However, relapses that happen during recovery should be disclosed to group members/spouse throughout the recovery process.

# THE ADDICT'S REALITY VS. THE SPOUSE'S REALITY

## THE ADDICT'S REALITY

- I'm becoming a person of integrity.
- I've never loved him/her more.
- I'm beginning to see how much I value our marriage.
- Finally, I'm an honest person.
- I understand the healing process sometimes takes three to five years. I'm sure I can complete this process in a couple of years.

## THE SPOUSE'S REALITY

- I've been betrayed.
- I've never felt less loved, worthy, or respected.
- I've never realized until now how little our marriage meant to him/her.
- How could he/she live a lie like this?
- Five years seems like a lifetime to deal with this pain.

Recognizing that these feelings are a normal part of the healing process allows both spouses to have grace for one another.

# STEPS TOWARD BUILDING TRUST

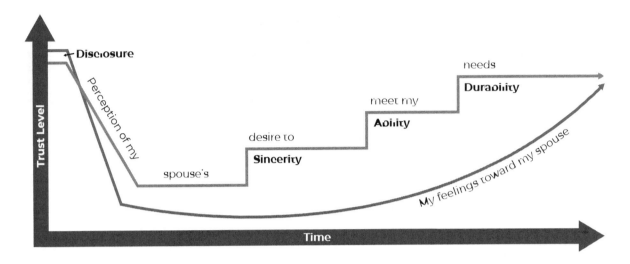

This chart is useful in describing various relationships where trust has been broken, not just in romantic relationships.

**Sincerity** is all about remorse. When a person is truly sorry for breaking trust.

**Ability** refers to the ability to meet others' needs or the ability to recover from breaking trust.

Where many couples get stuck is between ability and durability. The individual who broke trust is working really hard and the betrayed spouse is not able to trust yet.

**Durability** is about doing the hard work—both the struggler and the betrayed are doing their group work, using the tools, and trusting the process.

# RECOVERY ACTION PLAN

The Recovery Action Plan is intended for use following a relapse. Having a plan in place is helpful for both those struggling and those betrayed.

**For the addict:** creates a plan to maintain sobriety and move forward in recovery.

**For the betrayed:** creates a plan to help them continue making proactive choices and move forward in their healing.

The Recovery Action Plan relieves much of the anxiety felt by those betrayed but also for those who struggle. For those who are single, this tool should be used in partnership with their group or a mentor. They would make their commitments to the group or mentor.

This all starts with identifying relapse.

## NATURAL CONSEQUENCES

**Determine Natural Consequences:** consequences that personally affect both those struggling and those betrayed, without anyone imposing the consequence. This is not meant to be punitive, but asking what each individual spouse needs to continue in their healing.

**Examples:**

- **Married addict:** When I relapse it breaks trust with my spouse, increases the risk of exposure to my kids, and causes my spouse to feel unwanted and unneeded.
- **Betrayed spouse:** When my spouse relapses it causes me to feel like I am not enough, breaks my trust, increases my anxiety, and causes me to withdraw.
- **Single addict:** When I relapse, it causes me to feel shame and isolate from others.

## LOGICAL CONSEQUENCES

**Determine Logical Consequences:** consequences that are a reasonable and necessary outcome imposed personally or by another.

**Examples:**

- **Married/Single addict:** "What do I need to do to build back restoration & recovery?"
- **Betrayed spouse:** "What do I need to feel stable and be able to trust again?"

# PARENTING DYNAMICS

## WE CANNOT DEAL WITH THE PRESENT UNLESS WE UNDERSTAND HOW WE WERE AFFECTED IN THE PAST.

As parents, when we get healthy, it changes the culture, environment, and the way we communicate in our home. Whether we have children in the home or adult children, it is never too late to create healthy change in relationships.

A healthy person knows what their issues are, can articulate them, and what they're doing to work on it.

# SHARING OUR STORY

> They triumphed over him by the blood of the Lamb
> and by the word of their testimony;
>
> REVELATION 12:11

No one else has our testimony. No one else can speak to what God has done in our lives.

Owning our story and testifying to what God has done in our lives through our healing is what provides the change, the hope, and the encouragement for others.

_____

_____

_____

_____

_____

# Session 07.

# REFLECTION QUESTIONS

**?** | Why is understanding the difference between Unhealthy Sexuality and Healthy Sexuality an important part of the healing process for both spouses?

_____

_____

_____

_____

_____

**?** | Disclosure is a tough subject. Allowing the addicted spouse time to process and make sense of their sexual history takes time. How is this beneficial for both spouses during the recovery process?

_____

_____

_____

_____

_____

**?** While waiting for disclosure, what assurance does a betrayed spouse have that their spouse is doing all the right things to find healing?

_____

_____

_____

_____

_____

_____

**?** When looking at The Addict's Reality vs. The Spouse's Reality chart, how does this explain the perspective of both spouses? Through the group process, how do we help them see their spouses perspective?

_____

_____

_____

_____

_____

_____

**?** Rebuilding trust takes time. If we have been betrayed by someone, what behaviors should we look for when measuring sincerity, ability, and durability?

_____

_____

_____

_____

_____

_____

**?** | How might having a Recovery Action Plan in place help a person avoid relapse? How does a Recovery Action Plan help a spouse in their response when a relapse occurs?

_____

_____

_____

_____

_____

_____

_____

_____

_____

_____

_____

**?** | How successful were you in using the FASTER Scale last week? What did you learn about yourself through this exercise? What did you find confusing?

_____

_____

_____

_____

_____

_____

_____

_____

_____

_____

_____

*Session 07.*

# WEEKLY WORK

# RECOVERY ACTION PLAN

An action plan is a document that lists what steps must be taken in order to achieve a specific goal. Benjamin Franklin once said, "*If you **fail to plan**, you are **planning to fail**.*"[2] The **Recovery Action Plan** is a good tool for anyone wanting to take a proactive approach to their recovery and their relationships.

The goal is to re-establish trust and to implement actions that need to be taken in order to process the relapse and trauma in an positive, intentional manner.

**Keep in mind:** You will develop a Recovery Action Plan for *yourself*. If your spouse gets to the point in recovery where he or she has created his/her own Recovery Action Plan, you will add your Recovery Action Plan to his/hers. The addict spouse creates a Recovery Action Plan up front to provide guardrails and accountability during the initial stage of recovery. However, when the betrayed spouse presents his/her Recovery Action Plan, that will become the Recovery Action Plan for your marriage— the plan for you and your spouse. If your spouse is not in a Pure Desire group, the Recovery Action Plan you created for yourself—with your group—will continue to provide parameters and accountability for you.

---

[2] Goodreads. (2013, June 22). *Quote by Benjamin Franklin.* Retrieved from https://www.goodreads.com/quotes/460142-if-you-fail-to-plan-you-are-planning-to-fail

→ Before the disclosure, there were probably secrets in the relationship. Because of this, it will be difficult for your spouse to trust your words or their own instinct. Your spouse must SEE things that will help them start trusting again. Your spouse is learning to believe behaviors and not just words. Create a plan together to rebuild (or maintain) trust and intimacy.

→ **For single group members:** For a married person, it's easier to see the hurt their spouse and family experiences when he or she confesses a relapse, but for a single person, it's not that simple. In most cases, single people have little experiential understanding of how their sexual behavior affects others and themselves. It is crucial that you begin to associate your sexual acting out with logical consequences and learn how to develop healthy intimacy as a single person.

→ **For group members who are separated or divorced:** Your *Recovery Action Plan* will provide additional boundaries and direction in dealing with co-parenting—establishing individual and relational health—regardless of the marriage outcome.

Having consequences decided ahead of time will allow you to fall back on your plan when relapse occurs instead of allowing emotions to take the wheel.

# IDENTIFY NATURAL AND LOGICAL CONSEQUENCES

→ A **natural consequence** occurs as a result of a choice without anyone imposing it.

→ A **logical consequence** is a reasonable and necessary outcome imposed personally or by another.

# RECOVERY ACTION PLAN STEPS FOR THE ADDICT

**01.** Identify your relapse.

**02.** Determine who you need to share your relapse with, and in what time frame.

**03.** Write out all the **natural** consequences of your relapse.

**04.** Write out a list of **logical** consequences you choose to follow if you relapse.

**05.** Review your **escape plan** or create one by visiting puredesire.org/tools.

**06.** Describe your desired outcome for creating this plan.

**Full Recovery Action Plans, with examples, can be found at puredesire.org/tools.**

# REBUILDING TRUST

**?** | What is a relationship you have where you are working to build/rebuild trust with them?

_____

_____

**?** | How are you showing sincerity?

_____

_____

_____

**?** | How are you making it clear that you have the ability to be trusted?

_____

_____

_____

_____

**?** | What will it take to show durability to this commitment?

_____

_____

_____

_____

# Session 08.
# HEALING WOUNDEDNESS

If we want to live fully in sexual health, we need to make sense of our unprocessed trauma—how our painful past experiences continue to show up in our daily lives. How are the wounds from our past interfering with our relationship with God and others?

In this session, we talk through several stages of the healing process and what it practically looks like to live in freedom.

Pursuing health allows us to be close—create relationships—with the people in our lives. Our approach in looking at our past and looking at our wounds is not to blame someone.

For many of us, our families, our parents, our caregivers loved us and did the best they could...and they hurt us. These are not mutually exclusive ideas.

Being able to process through our past and our pain allows us to better love the people in our lives, even the people who hurt us.

**WE CAN ONLY WORK ON THE PROBLEMS WE OWN.**

We can't work on the problems we're still blaming on someone else. Our perspective needs to be focused on owning our current struggles—regardless of what we experienced or if others around us are unwilling to change—so we can move forward in our healing and become who God has called us to be.

_____

_____

_____

_____

_____

_____

_____

_____

_____

_____

When it comes to healthy sex and sexuality, the real battle is not between our legs, it's in our brain.

## WE BATTLE AGAINST THE LIES OF HELL THAT HAVE BEEN ROOTED IN OUR SOULS THROUGH TRAUMA.

# TYPES OF TRAUMA

➡ **Trauma of infringement (Big T):** trauma done to us, typically one-time experiences, which is all about intensity.

➡ **Trauma of abandonment (Little t):** trauma due to things kept from us or things that happen to us consistently over time, which is all about frequency.

**Infringement**

- Combat experiences
- Rape
- Sexual abuse
- Punching
- Slapping
- Verbal attacks
- Demeaning nicknames

Intensity

Extreme

Moderate

Mild

Frequency

**Abandonment** → Silence → Neglect → Lack of support → Open rejection

# PRINCIPLES OF TRAUMA

## 01. WE HAVE BEEN WOUNDED IN RELATIONSHIPS.

## 02. UNPROCESSED WOUNDS OR TRAUMA CREATE ISOLATION.

## 03. TIME DOES NOT HEAL ALL WOUNDS.

> "IF WE DON'T TURN AND FACE OUR TRAUMAS, IF WE DON'T TURN
> AND MOURN SOME OF THE HEARTACHES OF OUR LIFE,
> WE ARE GOING TO TRY TO FIND ALMOST ANYTHING THAT
> WE CAN FIND COMFORT AND ESCAPE."
>
> JAY STRINGER

## 04. WE ARE HEALED IN RELATIONSHIP WITH GOD AND OTHERS.

# NEW EXPERIENCES OF LOVE AND GRACE REPLACE THE TRAUMA OF OUR PAST.

This can happen through a recovery group, in counseling, or with a spouse.

## "59% OF PEOPLE STRUGGLING WITH UNWANTED SEXUAL BEHAVIOR DID NOT HAVE ANYONE TO TALK TO WHEN STRUGGLING."

### JAY STRINGER

When we experience fear and feel unsafe, it initiates our fight-flight-or-freeze response. This is often an indication that we have unprocessed trauma in our lives.

**?**

01. What situations push your buttons or cause you to overreact? (Initiate a fight response?)

02. What situations do you fear most or withdraw from? What causes you the most worry? (Initiate a flight response?)

03. What situations cause you to feel paralyzed or that you have to make others happy? (Initiate a freeze or appease response?)

04. Looking at your answers to the previous questions, what does this reveal to you about your sources of trauma?

Processing our trauma and moving toward health isn't linear, it's cyclical.

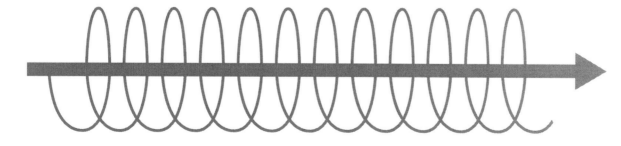

There may be times when we think we've processed through our trauma, but then a new nuance of the trauma presents itself, so we have to process through it again. The process of health and recovery, or working through betrayal, is not about answering a question and moving on. It's a process of working on progress, not perfection.

# THE FOUR STAGES OF THE HEALING PROCESS

## 01. REBOOTING

If we're going to deal with our trauma, we need to know what our triggers are so they can be rebooted. When we don't talk through our trauma, it stays in our soul and festers.

> **Action Step:** we need to process the sources of our trauma with a trusted advisor.

# 02. ACCEPTANCE

If we're going to be working on our woundedness, we need to accept what's been going on.

The opposite of acceptance will halt progress: this is denial.

**The Five Emotional Stages of Healing:**

**01.** Crisis/Decision

**02.** Shock

**03.** Grief

**04.** Repair

**05.** Growth

> **!**  **Action Step:** we need to write down our current reality and how we will prevail—what hope looks like to move forward.

# 03. INTEGRATION

This is like peeling back the layers of an onion. The treatment process or moving toward health and healing is gradual; it takes time.

In integration, we need to reframe the pain. We can't move through this healing process unless we are willing and able to feel the pain that's there in order to heal it.

> **!**  **Action Step:** determine our prophetic or personal promises and rehearse them daily.

### Personal/Prophetic Promises

This approach allows God to show us who we are, how He sees us, and connect this to experiences we've had in life, so we can see where we're headed; as opposed to being crippled and sidelined by the lies that have come out of the trauma we've experienced.

## IN ORDER TO RENEW THE MIND, WE NEED TO EXPERIENCE GOD SO THE LIMBIC LIES ARE OVERCOME!

**Experiencing God**

?

01. When have you personally experienced God?

02. What was God saying to you about you in that experience?

03. What promise in Scripture could you link to this experience?

04. How does this truth directly counteract a limbic lie?

## WE CAN'T CHANGE OUR HISTORY, BUT WE CAN CHANGE THE LIES ATTACHED TO OUR HISTORY.

# 04. RESTORATION

This is the process of moving into our God-given future, becoming or living as the person we were created to be. This is not a straight line, but a process that takes constant course correction; allowing us to move more and more toward health and who God has called us to be.

**FORGIVENESS**     passing on the grace we have experienced.

## DIVINE REVERSAL

God can use what the enemy brought against us to bless others instead.

> *All praise to God, the Father of our Lord Jesus Christ. God is our merciful Father and the source of all comfort. He comforts us in all our troubles so that we can comfort others. When they are troubled, we will be able to give them the same comfort God has given us.*

**2 CORINTHIANS 1:3-4 NLT**

> **!**    **Action Step:** pay it forward.

> ## "THE POINT OF YOUR GREATEST WOUNDEDNESS IS WHERE YOU ARE THE MOST GIFTED.
> ### DR. TED ROBERTS

# Session 08.

# REFLECTION QUESTIONS

**?** | Why is it important to look at our wounds, as a component of our healing process?

_____

_____

_____

_____

**?** | When thinking of trauma, what type of experiences come to mind? How does Robert's description of trauma help us understand the impact small but frequent types of trauma have on addictive behaviors?

_____

_____

_____

_____

_____

_____

**?** | How does identifying our triggers help us recognize
areas of unprocessed trauma?

_____

_____

_____

_____

_____

**?** | Describe in your own words a prophetic or personal promise.
Why is discovering our prophetic or personal promise a crucial step
in the healing process?

_____

_____

_____

_____

_____

**?** | In what ways has this session prepared you to help others find healing?

_____

_____

_____

_____

**?** | After creating a Recovery Action Plan last week,
what questions do you have?

_____

_____

_____

_____

# WEEKLY WORK

# TRAUMA CHECKLIST

**01.** Did you have any medical problems or hospitalization early in life. ········· ☐ Yes ☐ No

**02.** I get easily lost in my work. ························· ☐ Yes ☐ No

**03.** I have periods of sleeplessness. ····················· ☐ Yes ☐ No

**04.** I feel bad at times about myself because of shameful experiences in my past.
☐ Yes ☐ No

**05.** I have trouble stopping certain actions even though they are unhelpful/destructive.
☐ Yes ☐ No

**06.** My relationships are the same story over and over again. ········· ☐ Yes ☐ No

**07.** I was adopted. ······································· ☐ Yes ☐ No

**08.** I am unable to recall details of painful experiences. ··········· ☐ Yes ☐ No

**09.** I avoid mistakes at all costs. ······················· ☐ Yes ☐ No

**10.** Unsettling thoughts or memories have come to mind out of the blue. ☐ Yes ☐ No

**11.** Sometimes I have outbursts of anger or irritability. ··········· ☐ Yes ☐ No

**12.** Sometimes I spoil opportunities for success. ················ ☐ Yes ☐ No

| 13. | There is something destructive I do over and over, starting early in my life. | ☐ Yes | ☐ No |
| 14. | I have difficulty concentrating. | ☐ Yes | ☐ No |
| 15. | Growing up I was separated from one or both parents or my siblings for a long time. | ☐ Yes | ☐ No |
| 16. | My parents fought a lot verbally and/or physically. | ☐ Yes | ☐ No |
| 17. | We moved a lot when I was growing up. | ☐ Yes | ☐ No |
| 18. | I am a risk taker. | ☐ Yes | ☐ No |
| 19. | I stay in conflict with someone when I could have walked away. | ☐ Yes | ☐ No |
| 20. | I often feel sexual when I am lonely. | ☐ Yes | ☐ No |
| 21. | I feel loyal to people even though they have hurt me. | ☐ Yes | ☐ No |
| 22. | I feel I must avoid depending on people. | ☐ Yes | ☐ No |
| 23. | I use TV, reading, eating and hobbies as a way of numbing out. | ☐ Yes | ☐ No |
| 24. | I have a problem with putting off certain tasks. | ☐ Yes | ☐ No |
| 25. | I need lots of stimulation so that I don't get bored. | ☐ Yes | ☐ No |

**Enter the number of "yes" you marked**

# PERSONAL PROMISES

Based on what you learned in this session about personal promises and times when you've experienced God, identify two personal promises that help you remember who God created you to be.

**01.**

**02.**

*Bonus Session*

# RUNNING GROUPS AT YOUR CHURCH

_____

_____

_____

_____

_____

_____

_____

_____

_____

_____

_____

_____

_____

_____

_____

_____

_____

# APPENDIX

# NEXT STEPS

So what now? The worst thing to do with all of this time, teaching, and tools is to do nothing. Here's what we suggest:

## JOIN A GROUP

Find a local or online group through the Pure Desire website and start your healing journey. Whether you're struggling or betrayed, a group is the best next step.

→ Visit **puredesire.org/join-a-group** to join a group.

## START GROUPS IN YOUR CHURCH/COMMUNITY

Don't wait any longer. People in your church are struggling, they're hurting, and they need a safe place to go to process their behavior and find freedom from it. And, we can help you get started.

→ Don't miss the bonus disk on Starting Groups In Your Church.

→ After watching *Sexual Integrity 101* as a church leadership team (staff and ministry leaders), contact our International Group Coordinators at groups@puredesire.org to discuss your specific circumstances, challenges, and needs.

## GET ADDITIONAL TRAINING

Check out our Pure Desire podcast for weekly teaching, training, and encouragement. Or, come to a Pure Desire Event or Regional Group Training.

→ Listen at **puredesire.org/podcast** or on iTunes, Google Play, Spotify, and Stitcher.

→ Visit **puredesire.org/find-an-event** to find a training event near you.

## CONSIDER COUNSELING

Whether you are single or married, Pure Desire Counselors can walk you through your recovery or healing journey. **Over 90% of our counseling is done online**, so you can get counseling from wherever you are.

→ Visit **puredesire.org/counseling** for more information.

# CONTACT US

Reach out. Ask questions. Get encouragement for your next step on the healing journey. Or get trained by our staff on how to start groups in your church.

- Email us at **info@puredesire.org**.
- Call us at **(503) 489-0230**.
- Mail us at **886 NW Corporate Dr, Troutdale, OR 97060**.

The journey to lasting health is a long process. It can take 2-5 years of God doing miracles every single day.

This 8-week course is not the solution. It's just the beginning.

Don't sit on this. Stand up. Own your story. Pursue healing. Let's change the tide of sexual brokenness in our world.

We believe that if you lean into this process, if you implement the tools, and you trust that God will work through this process, great healing and change will happen for you and for those around you. God bless you on your healing journey.

# ACCOUNTABILITY SOFTWARE

Having the right accountability software is an essential tool in our recovery kit. Partnering in a safe, grace-filled group, we'll discover the freedom found with the right app—for us and our family.

## COVENANT EYES

Visit **coveyes.com/puredesire** to sign up for this accountability-based service: it's safe, secure, and proven effective at helping members overcome porn addiction.

## ACCOUNTABLE2YOU

Visit **accountable2you.com** for the most comprehensive accountability software tailored to your specific needs. Use the promo code: **PUREDESIRE**.

## EVER ACCOUNTABLE

Visit **everaccountable.com/pure-desire** for the most effective, simple way to help you make good choices online.

# PURE DESIRE GROUP GUIDELINES

These group guidelines were designed to create a safe environment for open and honest conversations during group meetings. Read and discuss the following guidelines as a group, including when anyone new joins the group:

- **Confidentiality:** What is said in the group is not shared outside the group.

- **Self-focus:** Speak only for yourself and avoid giving advice.

- **Limit Sharing:** Give everyone a chance to share.

- **Respect Others:** Let everyone find their own answers.

- **Regular Attendance:** Let your leader or co-leader know if you cannot attend a meeting.

- **Commitment to Accountability:** Make a minimum of three contacts a week. If you have relapsed in the last week, then a daily contact is recommended.

- **Listen Respectfully:** No side conversations.

- **Take Ownership and Be Responsible:** If you feel uncomfortable with anything, talk with your leader or co-leader, or your small group.

- **Stay on the Subject/Questions:** Watch those rabbit trails!

- **Homework Completion:** Allow 20-30 minutes per day to complete your homework. If you don't do your homework, you won't win your battle with healing, and you will not be able to participate when the group is processing their homework.

- **Covenant to Contend (CTC):** The CTC is an open commitment of accountability which states why you have chosen to join a PD small group and what you are committed to do in order to win your battle with sexual addiction. At the bottom of the page you will notice a place for you and one other person to sign and date. This is a public commitment. Read the CTC and ask a member of your group to sign as a witness to your signature.

- **Memo of Understanding:** This document indicates that you have read and understand the purpose and parameters of PD groups and the moral and ethical obligations of leaders.

# MEMO OF UNDERSTANDING

Please read and sign this memo, indicating that you have read and understand the purpose and parameters of Pure Desire groups and the moral and ethical obligations of the group facilitators.

I understand that every attempt will be made to guard my anonymity and confidentiality in this group, but that anonymity and confidentiality cannot be absolutely guaranteed in a group setting.

- I realize that the group facilitator cannot control the actions of others in the group.
- I realize that confidentiality is sometimes broken accidentally and without malice.
- I understand that I am allowed to share any of my personal experiences with others outside the group, however, I also understand that disclosing any information about others in the group with anyone outside the group is strictly prohibited. I understand that this type of behavior, whether intentional or unintentional, may result in termination of my group participation.

I understand that the group facilitator is morally and ethically obligated to discuss with me any of the following behaviors, and that this may lead to breaking of confidentiality and/or possibly intervention:

- I communicate anything that may be interpreted as a threat to self-inflict physical harm.
- I communicate an intention to harm another person.
- I reveal ongoing sexual or physical abuse.
- I exhibit an impaired mental state.
- I reveal that I have perpetrated an act of child abuse and/or child molestation or have expressed the intent to commit such an act.
- I reveal that I have perpetrated or am considering an abusive act toward the elderly/disabled.

I have been advised that the consequences for communicating the above types of information may include reports to the proper authorities - the police, suicide units, or children's protective agencies, as well as to any potential victims.

I further acknowledge that if I am on probation and/or parole and I engage in wrongful behavior in violation of my parole/probation, part of my healing/recovery may include notifying the appropriate authorities.

I understand that this is a Christ-centered group that integrates recovery tools with the Bible and prayer, and that all members may not be of my particular church background. I realize that the Bible may be discussed more (or less) than I would like it to be.

I understand that this is a support group and not a therapy group and that the group facilitator is qualified by "life experience" and **not** by professional training as a therapist or counselor. The group facilitator's role in this group is to create a climate where healing may occur, to support my personal work toward recovery, and to share their own experience, strength, and hope.

**Name** (please print) _____  **Date** _____

**Signature** _____

**PD Group Leader** _____  **Signature** _____

# MEN'S AROUSAL TEMPLATE EXAMPLE

| **Step 01:** The specific triggers and behaviors for me | **Step 02:** Early painful sexual relational experiences | **Step 03:** As a child, how did you feel and act? |
|---|---|---|
| **Risk:** Constant masturbation and fantasies | **5/6** Older sister attempted to have sexual intercourse | Fearful and excited |
| **Taboos:** Erotic writings on the Internet | **5/6** Began to masturbate | Shame and anger |
| **Quick and anonymous:** Frequent sexual encounters with anonymous males | | |
| ⊙ Tall, dark, and well-built | | |
| ⊙ Parks and public bathrooms | **7/8** Sister and relative attempt intercourse with me; discovered by mother | Alone |
| ⊙ Bath houses | | |
| ⊙ Porn shops | | |
| ⊙ Quick and dirty | | |
| **Secrecy:** Sexually anorexic with wife | **Jr. High** Mother discovered sister in bed with me | Hurt and anger |
| **Non-relational:** Foul language is a turn-on—at work and in public | **High School** Forced to have oral sex with male student at knife-point | Isolated and used |

| Looking at Steps 1-3 | Step 04: Your overall themes and core beliefs | Step 05: Arousal patterns, triggers, and recovery strategies |
|---|---|---|
| | | **Inner Circle** |
| *01.* How do they make you feel? | *I am worthless* | |
| *02.* Why do you violate biblical standards (taboos)? | *Breaking taboos is exciting* | |
| | | **Middle Circle** |
| *03.* How does this make you feel about those of the opposite gender? | *Can't trust women* | |
| | | **Outer Circle** |
| *04.* Why do you tend to isolate? | *Don't get close to anyone; they will hurt you* | |

# WOMEN'S AROUSAL TEMPLATE EXAMPLE

**Step 01:** The specific triggers and behaviors for me

*Interested in unavailable men*

*Chase me*

*Seduction*

*Flirting*

*Affair that is emotional & sexual*

*Fantasy*

*Instant messaging*

*Phone sex*

**Step 02:** Early painful sexual relational experiences

*Parents divorced at age 4*

*Terror from stepdad—age 6; chased Mom with a knife*

*Mom on couch w/ BF —age 7*

*Threatened to not tell about problems at home —ages 4 to 16*

*Lost virginity—age 16*

*BF left for college*

*Watched porn with BF —age 16*

*Escaped into fantasy life to survive*

*Affair with old BF after many years of marriage*

**Step 03:** As a child, how did you feel and act?

*Family members can't be trusted; they create feelings of abandonment & fear.*

*My fantasy world is safer than the real world.*

**Looking at**
Steps 1-3

**01.** *How do they make you feel?*

**02.** *Why do you violate biblical standards (taboos)?*

**03.** *How does this make you feel about those of the opposite gender?*

**04.** *Why do you tend to isolate?*

**Step 04:** Your overall themes and core beliefs

*I am worthless.*

*Breaking taboos is exciting.*

*Don't get close to anyone; they will hurt you.*

*I can't trust men.*

*The only safe place is living in fantasy.*

*I can't be alone.*

**Step 05:** Arousal patterns, triggers, and recovery strategies

**Inner Circle**

**Middle Circle**

**Outer Circle**

# RECOVERY ACTION PLAN

An action plan is a document that lists what steps must be taken in order to achieve a specific goal. Benjamin Franklin once said, "*If you **fail to plan**, you are **planning to fail**.*"[1] The **Recovery Action Plan** is a good tool for anyone wanting to take a proactive approach to their recovery and their relationships.

The goal is to re-establish trust and to implement actions that need to be taken in order to process the relapse and trauma in an positive, intentional manner.

**Keep in mind:** You will develop a Recovery Action Plan for *yourself*. If your spouse gets to the point in recovery where he or she has created his/her own Recovery Action Plan, you will add your Recovery Action Plan to his/hers. The addict spouse creates a Recovery Action Plan up front to provide guardrails and accountability during the initial stage of recovery. However, when the betrayed spouse presents his/her Recovery Action Plan, that will become the Recovery Action Plan for your marriage— the plan for you and your spouse. If your spouse is not in a Pure Desire group, the Recovery Action Plan you created for yourself—with your group—will continue to provide parameters and accountability for you.

⊙ Before the disclosure, there were probably secrets in the relationship. Because of this, it will be difficult for your spouse to trust your words or their own instinct. Your spouse must SEE things that will help them start trusting again. Your spouse is learning to believe behaviors and not just words. Create a plan together to rebuild (or maintain) trust and intimacy.

⊙ **For single group members:** For a married person, it's easier to see the hurt their spouse and family experiences when he or she confesses a relapse, but for a single person, it's not that simple. In most cases, single people have little experiential understanding of how their sexual behavior affects others and themselves. It is crucial that you begin to associate your sexual acting out with logical consequences and learn how to develop healthy intimacy as a single person.

⊙ **For group members who are separated or divorced:** Your *Recovery Action Plan* will provide additional boundaries and direction in dealing with co-parenting— establishing individual and relational health—regardless of the marriage outcome.

Having consequences decided ahead of time will allow you to fall back on your plan when relapse occurs instead of allowing emotions to take the wheel.

---

[1] Goodreads. (2013, June 22). *Quote by Benjamin Franklin*. Retrieved from https://www.goodreads.com/quotes/460142-if-you-fail-to-plan-you-are-planning-to-fail

# IDENTIFY NATURAL AND LOGICAL CONSEQUENCES

- ➲ A **natural consequence** occurs as a result of a choice without anyone imposing it.
- ➲ A **logical consequence** is a reasonable and necessary outcome imposed personally or by another.

# RECOVERY ACTION PLAN STEPS FOR THE ADDICT

**01.** Identify your relapse.

**02.** Determine who you need to share your relapse with, and in what time frame.

**03.** Write out all the **natural** consequences of your relapse.

**04.** Write out a list of **logical** consequences you choose to follow if you relapse.

**05.** Review your **escape plan** or create one by visiting puredesire.org/tools.

**06.** Describe your desired outcome for creating this plan.

# RECOVERY ACTION PLAN STEPS FOR THE SPOUSE

**01.** Identify what constitutes a relapse.

**02.** Determine who your spouse needs to share their relapse with, and in what time frame.

**03.** Write out all the **natural** consequences of your spouse's behavior.

**04.** Write out a list of **logical** consequences connected to the behavior that would help you see that your spouse recognizes the serious nature of their actions.

**05.** Make a list of steps you will need to personally take in order to find health and stability, and be ready to fully engage in the relationship.

**06.** Describe your desired outcome for creating this plan.

**Full Recovery Action Plans, with examples, can be found at puredesire.org/tools.**

# THE MAKING OF A SEX ADDICT

## Sexual Behavior

- Fantasy **18%**
- Voyeurism **18%**
- Exhibitionism **15%**
- Seductive Role Sex **21%**
- Intrusive Sex **18%**
- Anonymous Sex **18%**
- Trading Sex **12%**
- Paying for Sex **15%**
- Pain Exchange **16%**
- Exploitive Sex **13%**

## Other Addictions

- Chemical Dependency **42%**
- Eating Disorders **38%**
- Compulsive Working **28%**
- Compulsive Spending **26%**
- Compulsive Gambling **5%**

## Sexual Addiction

- Compulsive Behavior **94%**
- Loss of Control **93%**
- Efforts to Stop **88%**
- Loss of Time **94%**
- Preoccupation **77%**
- Inability to Fulfill Obligations **87%**
- Continuation Despite Consequences **85%**
- Escalation **74%**
- Social, Occupational, Recreational Losses **87%**
- Withdrawal **98%**

**Catalytic Environment
Catalytic Stress**

## Addiction Interaction

- Cross Tolerance **61%**
- Withdrawal Mediation **56%**
- Replacement **43%**
- Alternating Addiction Cycles **41%**
- Masking **45%**
- Ritualizing **41%**
- Intensification **61%**
- Numbing **54%**
- Disinhibiting **42%**
- Combining **46%**

## Family

- Addicts in Family **87%**
- Rigid Family System **77%**
- Disengaged Family System **87%**
- Rigid/Disengaged Family System **68%**

## Abuse/Early Trauma

- Emotional 97%
- Sexual 81%
- Physical 72%

## 8 Trauma Factors

- Reaction **64%**
- Pleasure **64%**
- Blocking **69%**
- Splitting **76%**
- Abstinence **45%**
- Shame **72%**
- Repetition **69%**
- Bonding **69%**

## Catalytic Environment
## Catalytic Stress

# SEXUAL ADDICTION SCREENING TEST (SAST-R V2.0)[1]

The Sexual Addiction Screening Test (SAST) is designed to assist in the assessment of sexually compulsive or "addictive" behavior. Developed in cooperation with hospitals, treatment programs, private therapists and community groups, the SAST provides a profile of responses that help to discriminate between addictive and non-addictive behavior.

→ To complete the test, answer each question by placing a check next to it if it is true for you.

→ Although the statements are written in the present tense, if the statements have ever applied to your life, then place a check next to that item.

→ Statements are considered false only if they have never been a part of your life. If in doubt, let your first reaction be your guide.

→ Please complete the scoring, filling out the Core Item Scale, the Subscales and the Addictive Dimensions on the page that follows the test. Pay close attention to your results on the Core Item Scale as a score of 6 or more indicates an addiction may be present.

**01.** Were you sexually abused as a child or adolescent? ☐

**02.** Did your parents have trouble with sexual behavior? ☐

**03.** Do you often find yourself preoccupied with sexual thoughts? ☐

**04.** Do you feel that your sexual behavior is not normal? ☐

**05.** Do you ever feel bad about your sexual behavior? ☐

**06.** Has your sexual behavior ever created problems for you/your family? ☐

**07.** Have you ever sought help for sexual behavior you did not like? ☐

**08.** Has anyone been hurt emotionally because of your sexual behavior? ☐

**09.** Are any of your sexual activities against the law? ☐

**10.** Have you made efforts to quit a type of sexual activity and failed? ☐

**11.** Do you hide some of your sexual behaviors from others? ☐

*© 2008, P. J. Carnes, Sexual Addiction Screening Test - Revised (Used by permission)*

**152** APPENDIX

12. Have you attempted to stop some parts of your sexual activity? ☐

13. Have you felt degraded by your sexual behaviors? ☐

14. When you have sex, do you feel depressed afterwards? ☐

15. Do you feel controlled by your sexual desire? ☐

16. Have important parts of your life (job, family, friends, leisure activities) been neglected because you were spending too much time on sex? ☐

17. Do you ever think your sexual desire is stronger than you are? ☐

18. Is sex almost all you think about? ☐

19. Has sex (or romantic fantasies) been a way for you to escape problems? ☐

20. Has sex become the most important thing in your life? ☐

21. Are you in crisis over sexual matters? ☐

22. The Internet has created sexual problems for me. ☐

23. I spend too much time online for sexual purposes. ☐

24. I have purchased services online for erotic purposes (sites for dating). ☐

25. I have made romantic or erotic connections with people online. ☐

26. People in my life have been upset about my sexual activities online. ☐

27. I have attempted to stop my online sexual behaviors. ☐

28. I have subscribed to or regularly purchased or rented sexually explicit materials (magazines, videos, books or online pornography). ☐

29. I have been sexual with minors. ☐

30. I have spent considerable time and money on strip clubs, adult bookstores, and movie houses. ☐

31. I have engaged prostitutes and escorts to satisfy my sexual needs. ☐

32. I have spent considerable time surfing pornography online. ☐

33. I have used magazines, videos, or online pornography even when there was considerable risk of being caught by family members who would be upset by my behavior. ☐

34. I have regularly purchased romantic novels or sexually explicit magazines. ☐

35. I have stayed in romantic relationships after they became emotionally abusive. ☐

**36.** I have traded sex for money or gifts. ☐

**37.** I have had multiple romantic or sexual relationships at the same time. ☐

**38.** After sexually acting out, I sometimes refrain from all sex for a significant period. ☐

**39.** I have regularly engaged in sadomasochistic behavior. ☐

**40.** I visit sexual bath-houses, sex clubs, or video/bookstores as part of my regular sexual activity. ☐

**41.** I have engaged in unsafe or "risky" sex even though I knew it could cause me harm. ☐

**42.** I have cruised public restrooms, rest areas, or parks for sex with strangers. ☐

**43.** I believe casual or anonymous sex has kept me from having more long-term intimate relationships. ☐

**44.** My sexual behavior has put me at risk for arrest for lewd conduct or public indecency. ☐

**45.** I have been paid for sex. ☐

| SCALES | ITEMS | CUT-OFF | MY SCORE |
|---|---|---|---|
| **Core Item Scale** | 1-20 | 6 or more | |
| **Internet Items** | 22-27 | 3 or more | |
| **Men's Items** | 28-33 | 2 or more | |
| **Women's Items** | 34-39 | 2 or more | |
| **Homosexual Men** | 40-45 | 3 or more | |
| **Preoccupation** | 3, 18, 19, 20 | 2 or more | |
| **Loss of Control** | 10, 12, 15, 17 | 2 or more | |
| **Relationship Disturbance** | 6, 8, 16, 26 | 2 or more | |
| **Affect Disturbance** | 4, 5, 11, 13, 14 | 2 or more | |

# RELATIVE DISTRIBUTIONS OF ADDICT & NON-ADDICT SAST SCORES

This instrument has been based on screenings of tens of thousands of people. This particular version is a developmental stage revision of the instrument, so scoring may be adjusted with more research. Please be aware that clinical decisions must be made conditionally since final scoring protocols may vary. A score of 6 or more on the Core Item Scale indicates an addiction may be present.

# LOVE ADDICTION EVALUATION

*Put a check next to any statements that describe you in the present or in the past.*

**01.** I am driven by one or more compulsions (relationships, sex, food, drugs, shopping, etc.). ☐

**02.** I think my self-esteem is low. ☐

**03.** I think that my happiness depends on having a loving relationship. ☐

**04.** I often fantasize to avoid reality or loneliness. ☐

**05.** I feel I need to be "good" enough to earn love from others. ☐

**06.** I will do almost anything for that desired loving relationship. ☐

**07.** I find it difficult to say "no" and set healthy boundaries, especially in relationships. ☐

**08.** I keep looking for a relationship to fill what is missing or lacking in my life. ☐

**09.** I find myself thinking that things will (or would) be better in this new relationship. ☐

**10.** I have always felt a distance and/or lack of love from my dad and/or my mom. ☐

**11.** I have a difficult time having an intimate relationship with God. ☐

**12.** I go from over- to out-of-control in relationships, sex, food, money, drugs, shopping, etc. ☐

**13.** I crave and fear intimacy at the same time. ☐

**14.** I have used sex to get love. ☐

**15.** I have used sex/seduction to dominate another person, be in control, or get what I want. ☐

**16.** I take responsibility for people, tasks, and situations for which I am not responsible. ☐

**17.** I find myself in relationships that echo my past abuse. ☐

**18.** I was sexually abused as a child or adolescent. ☐

**19.** I have stayed in romantic relationships after they became abusive. ☐

**20.** I often find myself preoccupied with sexual thoughts or romantic daydreams. ☐

**21.** I have trouble stopping my sexual behavior when I know it is inappropriate. ☐

**22.** I have hurt others emotionally because of my sexual/romantic behavior. ☐

**23.** I feel bad at times about my sexual behavior. ☐

**24.** I have worried about people finding out about my sexual activities. ☐

**25.** I feel controlled by my sexual desire or fantasies of romance. ☐

**26.** I have been sexually or romantically involved with inappropriate people. ☐

**27.** When I have sex or am involved in sexual activity, I often feel depressed afterward. ☐

**28.** I have become emotionally or sexually involved with people I don't know. ☐

**Total Number of Items Checked**

If you scored a total of 3-6 items checked, we recommend going through the *Seven Pillars of Freedom* Kit (for men) or *Unraveled* Kit (for women). If you scored over 6 checked items, we recommend seeking counseling from a certified sexual addiction therapist. For more information and resources visit www.puredesire.org.

# PURE DESIRE RESOURCES

## GROUPS MATERIALS

### Behind the Mask

**Products Include:** *Behind the Mask* and *Behind the Mask Leader's Guide*

*Behind the Mask* provides practical strategies that can help young women move into sexual health. In this challenging season of your life, the biblical principles, clinical tools, and recent discoveries about the brain will allow you to walk in the freedom your heart has longed for.

### Betrayal & Beyond Kit

**Contains:** *Betrayal & Beyond Workbook* and *Betrayal & Beyond Journal*

The *Workbook* provides betrayed women with valuable tools, biblical wisdom, and testimonies by other courageous women who found hope, help, and encouragement. The companion *Journal* helps promote the daily commitment to self-care and emotional health.
**A *Leader's Guide* is available separately.**

### Conquer Series

**Products Include:** *Conquer Series 6-DVD Set Volume 1, Conquer Series 6-DVD Set Volume 2, Conquer Series Study Guide Volume 1, Conquer Series Study Guide Volume 2, Conquer Series Journal,* and *Conquer Series Leader's Guide*

The *Conquer Series* is a 10-week cinematic teaching series on sexual purity. Use the *Conquer Series Study Guide Volume 1 & 2* to provide powerful tools that help you set up proper boundaries, identify emotional triggers, and process personal shame. The *Conquer Series Journal* includes weekly tools and practices to produce weekly self-awareness on your journey to sexual integrity.

### Unraveled Kit

**Products Include:** *Unraveled* and *Unraveled Weekly Tools*

Through the use of personal stories, strategic tools and exercises, and weekly self-care lessons, *Unraveled* will become our guide. We will discover the core of our distorted beliefs, address the shame that drives our behaviors, and write a new ending to our story, crafted with hope and purpose.

## Hope For Men

*Hope for Men* is a workbook for men who have experienced betrayal. Most men would react in anger in order to cover up their fears and run from the pain. This workbook will prove that you are not alone and that hope and healing from sexual betrayal is possible.

## Living Free Kit

Contains: *Living Free Workbook* and *Living Free Journal*

*Living Free* is a resource for college-aged men that helps individuals identify and understand the underlying factors that create and reinforce habitual sexual behavior. The *Workbook* is a two-semester format that includes tools and lessons to help you experience greater intimacy with Jesus and others. The *Journal* includes practical tools that help develop healthy sexuality on a daily basis. **A *Leader's Guide* is available separately.**

## Seven Pillars of Freedom Kit

Contains: *Seven Pillars of Freedom Workbook*, *Seven Pillars of Freedom Journal*, and *Pure Desire*

*Seven Pillars of Freedom* is designed to provide a safe and focused format to process addiction, build a lifestyle of accountability, and find healing. The *Workbook* includes instructions and exercises to create structure for freedom and provide the biblical truth necessary to build on. The *Journal* provides tools that reinforces the daily commitment to self-care and personal health, which is vital to sobriety and spiritual growth. **A *Leader's Guide* is available separately.**

## Top Gun

*Top Gun* provides young men the practical steps necessary to move into sexual health as part of a unique team of fellow warriors. Together you'll study biblical principles and how they relate to the most recent research on sexual struggles. You'll develop strategies for success in purity and live out proven techniques. You'll stop hiding in shame as you learn to live strong and free.

# INDEPENDENT STUDY/MARRIAGE MATERIALS

### Connected

God designed marriage to reflect the love, passion, and intimacy He has for us. He wants the very best for you and your marriage. *Connected: Building a Bridge to Intimacy* was created to be used as a weekly study for you and your spouse. Together, you'll learn how to be intentional in your behavior toward your spouse, cultivating a relationship fueled by compassion, grace and love.

### Going Deeper

**Products Include:** *Going Deeper*, *Going Deeper Study Guide*, and *Going Deeper Leader's Kit*

We all want to know God better. We desire to go deeper—but how do we sort through the contradictory and sometimes extreme teachings in the church today? Ted Roberts joins best-selling author, Pam Vredevelt, to walk you step-by-step through eight distinctive ministries of the Holy Spirit.

### Sexy Christians

**Products Include:** *Sexy Christians*, *Sexy Christians DVD*, and *Sexy Christians Workbook*

In *Sexy Christians*, you will learn why men and women see sex so differently, what the greatest aphrodisiac is, and how to avoid the most lethal killer to a great sex life. You'll also discover what men's and women's sexual needs are and why they are so different, what sex is all about from God's perspective, and what the differences are between male and female sexual response cycles.

# COURSES

**Products Include:** *Sexual Integrity 101 Video Course* and *Sexual Integrity 101 Workbook*

*Sexual Integrity 101* is an 8-week training course intended to raise awareness of sexual brokenness. It's for men, women, students, pastors, lay leaders, parents, and more—anyone who wants to find freedom from the effects of unwanted sexual behaviors, betrayal trauma, and unhealthy relationship patterns.

# BOOKS

### Digital Natives

*Digital Natives* gives a glimpse into not only the workings of the Internet, but how the church culture is uniquely prone to be ensnared in destructive, online behavior. It answers the question, "How can we positively influence the next generation?"

### Exposed

*Exposed* is an account of James and Teri Craft's harrowing, yet beautiful journey through the devastating impact of sexual addiction. They each share their perspective of restoration after a single moment in time seemingly shatters their life, family, and careers. Walk with the Crafts on a practical and life-altering path to victory through a Christ-centered commitment to recovery, renewal, and restoration.

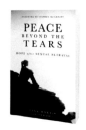

### Peace Beyond the Tears

Did you feel all alone when you discovered your husband's secret battle? Have you watched your marriage intimacy erode? Tina Harris has experienced those feelings—feeling like your world is falling apart, not knowing which way was up, and thinking something must be wrong with you. You are not alone. As Tina shares her story of pain and struggle, you will begin to see how God weaves together His grace with the pain of betrayal to bring healing.

### Pure Desire

*Pure Desire* is the answer to the desperate cry for help from men and women who have tried to build sexual holiness into their lives and failed...and failed...and failed. Chronicling the life of Dr. Ted Roberts, *Pure Desire* shows that hope is available by establishing healthy personal boundaries with proven, practical applications to claim Christ's healing power and presence, perhaps for the first time.

### Safe

Becoming a safe place will rarely happen by accident. It must be created by those who know the way; those who have walked a path of grace and know how to call others down that same road. *Safe: Creating a Culture of Grace in a Climate of Shame* provides the practical steps and tools needed to revive a passion for grace in the body of Christ.

### Setting Us Free

Have you ever found yourself thinking, *This isn't a big deal. All guys struggle with this kind of thing.* But at the same time feeling *I hope she never finds out. I always have something to hide.* As Nick shares his experience with these thoughts, you will discover how God shows up in unexpected ways and places to bring true and lasting freedom. This isn't just another how-to book on trying to control your behavior. This is the story of redemption.

### Stories for Men

This collection of *Stories for Men* provides insight into the lives of men who have struggled with sexual addiction and an understanding of the way isolation, shame, and loss accompany addictive behavior. Each has bravely chosen to take back what the enemy has stolen from them. Men from all walks of life have fearlessly taken on the challenge of writing their inspirational stories that you may find hope.

### Stories for Women

This collection of *Stories for Women* provides a unique approach to understanding the way sexual addiction impacts individual lives. Women from all seasons of life have taken on the challenge of writing their inspirational stories. Each has courageously chosen to take back what the enemy has stolen from them and write their stories for your strength and encouragement.

### The Forgiveness Factor

In this true story about one family's quest for restoration and wholeness, author Scott Bradley describes how forgiveness and restored relationships can come out of hurt, pain, and betrayal. Begin your journey of freedom as you read a raw, authentic story of hope and healing. You will also discover that the forgiveness factor can empower you to live a life full of purpose and meaning.

### The Silent Battle

Is your addiction taking over your life? Do you feel hopeless and alone? Rich Moore knows what you are going through. Many people stand at the crossroad in life not knowing whether to come clean and unburden the guilt and shame or to continue living under the weight of the secrets. As Rich shares his healing journey, you will see that true healing takes place through the pain, not void of it. This one man's story will show you that you're not alone and that God is with you regardless of challenges you face.